W9-BZO-465

What Can A Dentist Teach You About

Business, Life & Success?

Discover Secrets to Achieving
TOTAL SUCCESS!

Dr. Joe Capista

Maxwell Publishing
P.O. Box 551
Pleasant Hill, Oregon 97455

Copyright © 2008 by Joe Capista, DDS
First Edition 2008
Manufactured in the United States of America

ISBN 978-0-9658159-5-6

1. Business 2. Success 3. Spiritual

COMPANIES, ORGANIZATIONS, INSTITUTIONS, AND INDUSTRY PUBLICATIONS: Special books can be created to fit specific needs for private labeling with your logo on the front cover and a personalized message printed inside. For more information, contact our Sales Department at 541.654.0426.

The author of this book does not dispense any medical advice. The intent of the author is only to inform in a general nature. In the event you use any of the information in this book for yourself, which is your right, the author and publisher assume no responsibility for your actions.

"You can have anything in life you want if you want it badly enough and are willing to pay the price."

Charlie Schaivo

This book is dedicated to everyone who has a desire to live the life of your dreams and the courage to fulfill your destiny.

Acknowledgements

To Anne, my wife, for being the BEST!

*To Charlie, my mentor, for teaching me almost
everything I know about life.*

*To Kathleen Gage, my coach, for believing
in me and making everything happen.*

*To Dennis and Becky Vasquez, my dental lab owners, for giving
me the opportunities to facilitate presentations for their clients
and for listening and allowing me to grow as a speaker.*

*To David Haines, my accountant and advisor, for listening and
supporting me with my book and speaking career.*

*To all of my wonderful patients who trusted me to make your
smiles beautiful. I love what I do because of you.*

To my incredible team members. You make it all happen.

*To my mother and father;
I love you, I respect you, I hold you in my heart.*

TABLE OF CONTENTS

INTRODUCTION

If you are like most people, you might be asking yourself, "What can a dentist teach me about business, life and success?" Many think a dentist gets out of dental school, opens his or her practice and goes home rich and happy. The sad reality is this is not at all true. It may have been that way 50 years ago, but today a dentist has the same challenges as any other business owner. We have to attract and keep customers; know how to market and sell; and provide quality customer service in order to become and stay profitable.

Dentists, just like any other business professional, have to follow certain principles to be successful both personally and professionally. Many dentists are successful in business but not in their personal life. Many business professionals are successful in their work, yet often lack balance or a happy life. Therefore, they don't have *TOTAL SUCCESS*.

The daily challenges for dentists are the competition with other dentists and for discretionary dollars. Dentists also deal with pressure from insurance companies to participate in their plans. As part of an insurance plan, we are required to accept a lower payment for our services and are not paid our normal fee. With a lower reimbursement rate comes the increased stress of having to see more patients per day in order to make the same amount of money. To be insurance independent, we must have a well-run practice.

Unless we follow certain principles and systems in our business it is hard to survive and be as successful as we want to be. Chances are this is the same in your industry.

The topic of business success and success in life excites me. This is the primary reason I wrote this book. I thoroughly enjoy sales and marketing and sharing principles that give success to your business and personal life. It's what drives me to wake up with passion and excitement every single day.

I didn't come from a privileged upbringing. As a matter of fact, my upbringing was pretty average. I was not the smartest man or born with great business skills. Quite the opposite. What I know I have learned from others.

Over the years, I have gained knowledge about what it takes to go from where you are to where you want to be. I love sharing this knowledge. I love speaking about it, writing about it, and mentoring others on it.

The second reason I wrote this book is that I love to teach this topic. Whether I am writing or speaking to a group of college students, CEOs, business owners, dentists or sales professionals, I love teaching about success principles.

I am keenly aware that by teaching these principles and keeping my focus on the topic, I will continually be forced to look at what I do, constantly improve and keep the knowledge fresh in my mind so that I will continue to be successful. The more I focus on it, the more I use it in my own life. The more I use it, the more successful I become. The more success I experience, the more others benefit.

This book is a great resource for anyone who wants to shape and control his or her destiny. Whether you own a business, run a business, work for yourself, work for other people or are in sales, you will benefit from the information I share in this book.

You have control over your destiny and within your personal life and career. The success we have within our job or business is dependent on what we do with it, not what the owner does with it. We often blame the owner, not ourselves, for not having our success.

These principles apply even if you work for someone else. Don't make the mistake of thinking because you work for someone else the information won't apply. This is not the case at all! In reality, we all work for ourselves.

This book is for anyone who wants to have success principles for their life; their work life, business life and personal life.

There are specific objectives for this book. Much of what I am going to ask you to do is simple, but not easy. However, they are doable and achievable. What I want most for you to have are:

- Easy to understand and apply principles to grow your business.
- Principles based on systems so you will have success in your business.
- Principles based on systems so you will have a successful personal life.
- The skills and resources to achieve *TOTAL SUCCESS* and have a happy life.
- To "get it" and "do it."

In this book, I will cover the importance of having

systems in place that will give predictable and consistent results in both your business and personal life. I will focus on the big picture: the relationship of your Product or Service to your Internal and External Marketing and the relationship of these to your Sales Calls and Presentations.

I will also focus on the importance of having and using mentors, controlling your thoughts and maintaining balance in life. You will also learn how balance in your personal life can affect success in your business. You will learn about the relationship of having balance in your life in order to achieve *TOTAL SUCCESS*.

As you read through the pages of this book, you will learn about my upbringing, how mentors changed my life, why goals are so important in gaining direction and clarity, how to set yourself up for success in your business, the importance of giving back and ultimately of having a vision for the future.

I am very committed to you "getting it" and using this information to take the steps needed to be successful in your job, business and personal life.

In order to have *TOTAL SUCCESS*, you must have success in your personal and business life. Success is fleeting at best if you have it in only one area but not another. For me and all my mentors who taught me about *TOTAL SUCCESS*, the result is a *happy life*. Isn't that what most people want — a happy life?

Thank you for choosing to read this book. I know that for most of us, time is very limited. I respect your decision to let me share insights that can — and will — influence your life when you choose to take them to heart.

It is not just about building a successful business; it is about building a successful life. A life you can be certain is one of *TOTAL SUCCESS*.

CHAPTER I

Father Melton Wasn't Always Right

My name is Joe Capista and I have a story to tell. It is the story of a boy from a working class family who lived in an average suburban Philadelphia neighborhood, struggled to get good grades in grammar school, and today is recognized as one of the most successful individuals in my industry. It is my personal story of success about living a life many people only dream of while finding a deep connection and purpose beyond my wildest imaginings. It is the story of success that goes beyond the material and delves into the spiritual. It is a story that continues to unfold.

Looking back, I realize the foundation for my success began with my father, mother and grandfather. My father didn't graduate from college, he worked in a factory, as did my grandfather who immigrated to the United States from Italy. My uncle was a doctor, but the rest of my father's siblings all worked in factories as well. One day my grandfather said to me, "I want to live long enough to see you go to college." It was important to my grandfather that my siblings and I made something of ourselves. He placed a high value on education and achievement. He was sick at the time and close to death. Sadly, he didn't live long enough to see me go to college.

Growing up, I saw my father work hard for everything we had. We lived a very modest lifestyle. We didn't do anything extravagant such as go out to dinner. I think it was partly because we didn't have a lot of money and because family dinners at home were more important. Our life was a life of basics.

In terms of monetary success, I guess you could say my dad never made a lot of money. However, I always saw my dad as successful. He is a success as a family man, is virtuous, a good person and had more than enough money to live his lifestyle. He is one of the most successful people I know.

My dad provided well for us with what little he did have. Although he never verbalized it, he instilled in us a work ethic that lives on to this very day; an ethic born out of generations of work and a future of possibility. My dad knew we all had a better chance to succeed than he had and to become something.

It may sound a bit old fashioned to say I succeeded at the request of my father, but I knew if I did not, he and my mother would be disappointed. The thought of disappointing both my mother and father was too much to bear. As I grew up, I chose many paths because I didn't want to disappoint my parents. I didn't get in trouble because I knew it would be a disgrace to the family or it would make my parents unhappy.

When I was dating my girlfriend, I'd tell people the best

form of birth control was what my mother would say to me as I was walking out the door: "Don't disgrace the family." I knew what she meant. "Don't disgrace the family" was a saying that followed me throughout my adolescence keeping me on the straight and narrow.

Although neither of my parents were college educated, my father is a very well read man. He has read more books than I have and embodies a wealth of knowledge that is rare in today's world. His expectation for his children was a silent dictate that we would succeed. We were to carve out a profession that allowed us to elevate our lifestyle beyond that of the previous generation. He had a way of instilling an understanding that we should become something better, we should be more successful and have a better lifestyle than he and my mother had.

Without a word, it was understood we would go to college. It wasn't a choice; we were going. Being born a Capista was a one-way ticket to the greatest ride on earth: success, freedom, wealth and, most importantly, living a life filled with love!

Looking back, I could have been almost anything I set my mind to. So why a dentist? Growing up in the late 50's and 60's, there were basic occupations men chose for a living. You became a teacher, an accountant, a lawyer, an engineer or a doctor. There weren't jobs in technology; half the jobs available to young people today did not exist when I was making my life decision about work.

I knew I didn't want to be an accountant, teacher, lawyer or an engineer, so I was left with becoming a doctor. I wasn't sold on being a doctor in the truest sense of the word. I had an uncle that was a medical doctor and I saw the way he worked. He worked endless hours and I knew I didn't want that. He made house calls attending to the sick and ultimately many of his patients died. I certainly didn't want any part of that!

Through a process of elimination, I was slowly approaching the profession of dentistry. You could say I backed into it. I had bad teeth as a child and saw the dentist a lot. I was also impressed by the fact our family dentist had a Cadillac.

Having the humble upbringing I did, I thought having a Cadillac was pretty neat. Nobody in my neighborhood had a Cadillac; nobody had anything better than an old Chevy, Ford or a Rambler. There weren't many luxury cars where we lived and the fact my dentist made enough money to drive a Cadillac definitely left an impression.

I was also intrigued by the construction aspect of dentistry. I always liked building things. As a dentist, it appeared you could excavate, drill and build, and people would pay for your skill. The thought of drilling a hole, putting something in it, and in return you got 8 or 10 bucks (remember — this was a number of years ago), was all I needed to know. Dentistry looked clean, nobody was dying and my parents would be proud. Sign me up!

My friends and family all knew that I wanted to be a dentist since I was a kid. Around fifth or sixth grade I'd proclaim, "I want to be a dentist!" At an early age, I began a mental process that paved the way for my date with destiny.

I can remember playing basketball with my friends at the age of 12. When we were tired of basketball, we would head to the park and fill in the holes in the picnic tables and trees with mud. Each hole looked like an opportunity to fill an imaginary cavity. I eagerly filled each hole with whatever kind of makeshift amalgamate Mother Nature had to offer.

Grade school fantasy led to high school academics. By

now I'm getting average grades; second honors most of the time. I'm not setting the world on fire and I'm not in the advanced placement courses, but I'm in good, solid courses.

Junior year rolls around and it's time to go to a guidance counselor. I'm challenged with the decision of which college and what major to select! With some big life decisions staring me in the face, I needed some help... or so I thought.

Growing up in a solid Catholic family, I attended a parochial school. With my vision for the future firmly set in my mind, I decided to talk to Father Melton, my high school guidance counselor. After all, who has greater insight than someone working on behalf of the Divine?

Early into my meeting I declared, "Father Melton, I think I want to be a dentist!" After a moment of contemplation, Father Melton said, "Well, Joe, I don't think that's a very good idea. Your College Board scores are only 1040, and a thousand is just getting by. To be a biology major your scores should be over 1100."

He continued with complete certainty, "If you go to college for biology, you'll probably have a very difficult time, if you can make it at all. You ought to think about being a teacher because you have good skills. That would be a good career, it's a nice job."

I respectfully said, "Thank you," and left his office. Quickly shaking off what felt like total rejection, I assured myself I would apply for college as a biology major. After all, I had wanted to be a dentist since the 5th grade and all that hole digging and imaginary teeth filling at the creek wasn't going to be for nothing.

Sure I was making the right decision, I applied to five different colleges, all local schools outside of Philadelphia where

I grew up. I was accepted to all five colleges, but only as a declared biology major by one school — La Salle University. My choice was clear, La Salle it was.

After the first semester at La Salle, I had whopping 2.5 GPA, which is not enough to get into dental school or any professional school for that matter. It was just the first semester and I was in big trouble.

I was at a crossroads. I had to decide if I was going to change what I wanted to do and change my goal, or do I change what I'm doing to get to my goal? I decided I was not going to change my goal, so I had to do something differently in order to achieve my dream. This one decision of changing behaviors rather than changing my goal was the cornerstone of many future decisions that have created the life I now enjoy.

What had to be done differently was adjusting the intensity of my commitment. That meant changing the way I studied. I was not partying every weekend or messing around, I was doing what I thought was a reasonably good job, but obviously my GPA didn't reflect that. I decided that what I was doing wasn't enough.

I told my girlfriend, Anne, who later became my wife, we had to change our dating times. Even though Anne and I loved seeing each other, we decided we would only go out one night a week and I would study the other six nights. I consciously put my nose to the grindstone. For the next three and a half years, I memorized everything that was put in front of me. I was so focused on what I wanted, I remember leaving the Thanksgiving table one holiday evening and studying from Thursday through Sunday night without a break. I just never gave up.

Biology was tough. Father Melton told me it would be. My class started with 150 students and every day someone would drop out; they would fail biology and ultimately change their major. I had a lot of tenacity and even though I felt like an underdog, I had people in my corner. I had a family that taught me honor and a girlfriend that supported my dream.

In the end, we ended up with 49 biology majors. With visions of my father, mother and grandfather swimming in my head, I held tight and ended up with a 3.1 GPA, which was just enough to get me into dental school.

I applied to five dental schools. I was only accepted at one: Temple University School of Dentistry. I'll never forget the day I learned of my acceptance. It was the first day of December, the day acceptance or rejection notices were received.

Many of my friends who were on their way to medical school knew how much trepidation I had and how hesitant I was to call home. With continual prodding from my peers, I held my breath and made the call.

I began the conversation with, "Mom, is there a letter from Temple?"

She said, "Yes."

With no speakerphones at that time, I repeated what my mother said for my friends. "Open it up, Ma."

She begins to read, "The admissions committee is pleased..." That was all we needed to hear.

My friends drug me to the closest bar, stopping on the way to run into our chemistry class shouting, "Capista got into dental school!" Even an underdog can rally the excitement of others; five students vacated chemistry class to join us at the bar. It felt great to be accepted!

When I say I was an underdog, what I mean is I had to work hard to get to where I was going. Failure was never an option and success was something I wanted at an early age, but that did not mean it was easy. I had to struggle, adjust, and continually look for ways to succeed. Even though success wasn't easy, something strange happened when I got to Temple University. I completed all four years finishing a semester early and 11th in my class, which placed me in the top 10%. I guess I made the right choice to listen to my heart.

Dental school marked the beginning of developing my skills. During your first year in dental school, you get your instruments. Part of the instrument package is your drill. When I got that first drill, it was as if someone had given me gold. I would stare at it, hold it and affirm, "Yes! I'm going to get to do this!" It was almost a surreal experience. I knew I was on my path. I just knew it and nothing could stop me from becoming a dentist.

Dental school was a lot like the Marines; it was very tough and not very nice during the training. At the time, the school employed a method of motivation by beating you down before they built you up. I'm sure they wanted to weed out those who only thought they wanted to go into dentistry and find those who were actually going to become a dentist no matter what.

During the first year they were really out to make your life miserable and I was determined not to let it affect me. I knew I was going to do well and I loved dental school. I did well academically and when it was time for a residency, I was accepted everywhere I had applied.

Anne and I were engaged a few days after I was accepted to dental school. We were married after my first year. Financially we were on a very tight budget. Anne was a nurse and worked very hard. She paid the bills while I held on and worked towards my dream.

During that time, we went to garage sales to buy

furniture and had to be frugal. Even though money was tight and all of our furniture was used, one day we decided to splurge for a new sofa and chair. This was a huge event for us. We felt like we were living the big time with that new sofa and chair!

Our very first apartment was in Clifton Heights where I grew up. It was on Baltimore Pike, the main street in our town, above a pizza parlor. August was a really hot month in that apartment. We had no air conditioning and the heat of the pizza ovens would continuously rise. That first year it was so hot, our parakeet died of heat exhaustion. One day we came home and he was dead in his cage. I have to wonder how Anne and I survived the heat ourselves!

The place smelled all the time and there were many mice running around. It was kind of crazy, yet we loved it. Even though money was tight, we were very happy and very in love. I would sit with Anne, put my arm around her and say, "Honey, one day you're going to have everything. A fine home, nice car, lots of money and anything you want. I promise." At that time, flying to the moon would have been more believable than living a life where we could have anything we wanted, but I just knew in my heart we would.

The first year we were married we would watch the black and white TV we found during one of our garage sales excursions. It was also the year of the 1974 Olympics. I told Anne we were going to get a color TV to watch the Olympics.

We spent something like $129 for this little Zenith color TV just to watch the Olympics. That was a lot of money back then. Buying the color TV was important to me because I wanted my wife to get a glimpse of what was possible and the kind of luxuries that were awaiting us.

Anne became pregnant towards the end of my senior

year in college and we had our first child, Joseph, while I was in my residency. This was an exciting but tough time. We needed more room so we moved to a two-bedroom apartment during my residency. That was a huge stretch for us at the time.

As I started my first year in private practice, we had to stretch again. We bought a small, single home. We also had our second child, Vanessa, when we lived there.

Before we got married, Anne and I would ride through an area called Rose Tree and look at these big, beautiful houses. The homeowners were manicuring their lawns on big lots and seemed so happy and successful.

It was during those rides through Rose Tree that I would tell Anne, "Honey, someday we're going to live here." I just knew it would happen. I never had a doubt. I would visualize the life I wanted. What is amazing is that this is where we now live. I live in the very neighborhood we used to drive through; the very neighborhood I would feel a pang of excitement rush through my body every time we drove through.

I did my residency at Philadelphia General Hospital. I was fortunate to be able to build great people skills at Philadelphia General because I worked with a very diverse cross-section of people, mostly the poor, prisoners and police officers. I learned about compassion and humanity; it opened my heart, which became an important part of my way of doing business and my success.

My residency at Philadelphia General Hospital was a great experience. Even though I was working long hours, little by little I was watching my dream become a reality. At that time I didn't know much about goals, I just knew I had a dream and it was coming true.

During that time, I also worked evenings for a dentist,

eventually buying his practice. Interestingly enough, his office was about a mile or two from where I grew up. I worked 60 to 70 hour weeks, including Friday nights and Saturdays.

The dentist I worked for was far from progressive. He was overly thrifty, had antiquated equipment and a big closet he had converted into a treatment room. You couldn't even fit a dental assistant in there and it didn't have an X-ray machine. When I needed an X-ray, I had to wait for the dentist to finish, then go in and take an X-ray of my patient. We had two employees: a front desk person and a dental assistant. That was it.

In spite of his shortcomings, he had a ton of patients, something many dentists don't have. I watched and learned. I saw how good he was with people and because of him, I understood I was in the people business, not the dental business.

During my first year as a dentist, I decided I wanted to make $50,000. This was in 1977. Fresh out of my residency, I reached my goal and made the $50,000. That was a lot of money back then. In today's terms, it would be well over $200,000. I felt like I had arrived because of the kind of money I was making. All the hard work and sacrifice was paying off.

At that time, being successful in a practice meant you were netting six figures. With $50,000 under my belt in year one, I knew year two would bring $100,000. I was determined to make my goal of six figures and I did. I felt as though I was living a dream. A self-directed dream, but a dream nonetheless.

People can lose site of what it takes to achieve the life of their dreams. There is always a tradeoff, but it can be well worth it. The last year of my life had been filled with many moments of satisfaction, amazement and gratitude. We were living a life most people only dreamt of and I knew I had just begun!

You may think I am a good businessman and I am smart. As you can see from my educational background, I am just not that smart. The fact is — and it's really important for you to realize this — what I know about the world of business I learned from people who taught me how to run a business.

Success has very little to do with intelligence or skills. It has more to do with the way you think, feel and act. Because I know how important this is, I talk about this throughout the book. This doesn't mean you don't have to have skills or a certain amount of intelligence, but in this case my success has come more from intuition and thinking, not just from my intelligence and skills.

FATHER MELTON
SUCCESS SUMMARY

1. Dreams and desires can sometimes be more powerful than skills and intelligence.
2. Don't change your goals, change what you are doing to accomplish your goals.
3. What is in your gut is more important than what is in your head.
4. Trust your instincts.
5. We all need certain skills and intelligence to succeed, but success has very little to do with skills or intelligence.
6. Success comes more from the way we think, feel, and act.
7. Follow your dreams.

CHAPTER 2

The Man Who Changed My Life

Over the years, my definition of success has changed. Who I was directly out of dental school and who I am today are as different as night and day. Early on, success was measured simply by how much money I made and what my earning potential was.

Even though I began almost immediately to make great money at that first dental practice, somewhere inside I knew there had to be more to this than what I was experiencing. At that point, I didn't know there was any other way to achieve my dreams other than what I was doing.

After my first couple of years in this practice, I thought I needed to get out. It was crazy working all these hours in cramped corners! The dentist I worked for already had a few heart attacks, yet he kept pushing himself.

I intuitively knew there had to be more to life than how much money I made and what I could buy with it, yet I kept feeling the pressure to keep striving for more. The greatest pressure came from my own self-expectations. Money was my measurement of success, self-worth and value; or so I thought. It would take years of soul searching, learning, exploring and self-discovery to realize it is a balanced approach to all we do that creates ultimate satisfaction, happiness and success.

One fellow I remember well from the first practice was a dental supply representative. I can remember him as if it were yesterday, talking to him during his sales visits. I would confide in him that something seemed to be missing.

He would always tell me, "Joe, don't leave here. He doesn't run it right. This is a gold mine; you just have to learn how to run it."

His words would ring in my head. I knew I wanted to make great money, but I didn't like the way the business was being run. Up to this point, his way of doing business was the only way I knew how to run a practice.

I was torn between staying and dealing with it or striking out on my own and possibly failing. I knew that if I left I would leave with no patients and it would take a long time to build a practice from nothing.

It was during this period I set some goals to learn a better way. I wasn't focused on goal setting at the time, so I did the best I could with what little knowledge I had. Goal setting wasn't something taught in dental school.

It was also during this period I had my first extremely evident experience of setting an intention and watching the result manifest. It wasn't too long after thinking about setting out on my own I was offered the opportunity to buy into the practice. Not only was I going to be a partner in the practice, I was about to meet one of the most influential people in my professional life.

A quiet and gentle man, Charlie Schaivo, entered my life. Charlie was an accountant and a very specialized consultant with an expertise in dental practice acquisitions.

During the transition, Charlie met with my partner and me on a monthly basis assisting us in our business skills. As the practice was growing, my partner was easing into retirement. This was the perfect opportunity to run the business my way full speed ahead. Now I was going to find out what I was really made of! With Charlie's help, great events were on the horizon.

Charlie was a very refined man who rarely dressed in other than a business suit, well-pressed shirt, polished shoes and hat. He continues this practice even now in his late 80's. He once jokingly told me, "Joe, I even cut my lawn in a suit." Charlie's quiet confidence, love of learning and joy for life was contagious. I liked being around him. I could listen to him for hours as he instilled his wisdom in me.

It was during this time Charlie became the main mentor in my life. Little did I realize how influential and instrumental to my success this man would be.

Initially, we didn't talk about the fact he was my mentor, that aspect of our relationship simply evolved. We met once a month from 1979 to 1998. Each time we met we spoke about the month, a little bit about what we were doing in the office, and a lot about personal success, personal growth, how to sell, and how to help people.

Charlie introduced me to some of the greatest thought leaders of the time like Earl Nightingale, Zig Ziglar, Denis Waitley, Og Mandino, Napoleon Hill, Dale Carnegie and many others. He taught me the importance of learning from and modeling others. This was a very important lesson for me. It was to be the cornerstone of my success.

Along with helping me with my work habits, Charlie also helped me develop my spiritual life. Even though I grew up with strong Catholic influences, I wasn't very committed to my spiritual well being. At that time I had no clue how essential a solid spiritual life was to my own success. Charlie opened up a new way of viewing spirituality through teaching me the importance of family and relationships, physical health, financial well-being, contribution to community and the importance of commitment in these areas.

Something I love and have been amused by about Charlie from the beginning is he had a gift for seeing in others what they couldn't see in themselves. One day as he was taking me to pick up my car, he looked at me and said, "Joe, I see you someday with a big practice, with multiple locations, lots of dentists and very successful."

I secretly wondered if he was nuts. Here I was working in a cramped practice, I could hardly even get the fillings to stay in and was worried about getting people numb, never mind having a business where I would have a large, successful practice.

Charlie had a way of instilling confidence and teaching you without you even knowing it. He saw something in me I couldn't see in myself. I suppose that is what a good mentor does; they can see our potential.

Charlie had a way of putting ideas in my mind and letting me know I should be doing them. He never questioned me to see if I was doing what he had recommended. He wasn't going to bug me about it. He would just remind me in his own gentle way that they were important.

The funny thing is, even though I didn't always act on his recommendations, when I did, amazing things happened. My life improved in all areas. There were many occasions where it took years before I would act on something he said. Although I have no regrets for how my life has been and I know I have been blessed beyond my wildest dreams, I have to wonder how much differently life would have been had I acted on some of Charlie's recommendations earlier.

I have known other people who would meet with Charlie and they wouldn't do anything he recommended. Charlie is the kind of person who willingly shared his knowledge with others. There were many people who just couldn't see the gifts he offered. I am absolutely certain if it weren't for Charlie's wisdom I would not be where I am at today.

Because of what I was now learning from Charlie, in a brief period of time I'd gone from simply dreaming of becoming a dentist to beginning to perfect my practice. My practice not only included my patients and staff, but I was now developing another kind of practice that covered all aspects of life. I was learning that skill and knowledge alone are not enough.

Charlie taught me that success in anything goes beyond the obvious. Although I needed a certain amount of skill and knowledge, my successes were coming from the way I would think, feel and act, coupled with intense emotion and a steadfast belief in "self."

He also taught me the importance of setting specific goals. Setting goals is not a hit and miss process for Charlie. It has always been systematic, deliberate and the cornerstone of every other aspect of creating a wildly successful, abundant, happy, and balanced life.

What he taught me about setting goals has been so

instrumental in my success that I would be remiss to not dedicate an entire chapter to the importance of goal setting. In essence, goals are about gaining direction, clarity and vision.

THE MAN WHO CHANGED MY LIFE
SUCCESS SUMMARY

1. Another person can change your life if they believe in you and you believe in you.
2. A mentor can often see in you what you cannot see in yourself.
3. Listen and act on advice from experts or from people who know more than you do.
4. A mentor's legacy will be realized in countless ways: through the beliefs you adopt, the thoughts you have and the actions you take.
5. Success comes from the way you think, feel and act, coupled with intense emotion and a steadfast belief in "self."
6. A good mentor can be instrumental in helping you to find ways to manifest your goals faster and more efficiently than if you go it alone.
7. To get results, you must take action.
8. A mentor creates accelerated learning.
9. The greatest gift you can give a mentor is the gift of mentoring another.
10. A mentor/mentee relationship can last a lifetime or be one that is only meant to last a short while.

Chapter 3

Direction, Clarity and Vision

In virtually every success course I have taken, goal setting is a cornerstone for achievement. Charlie was a big believer in setting goals. From almost the first time we met, Charlie tried to impress on me the importance of goals. Not only having goals, but also writing them down and reviewing and reading them on a very regular basis. Charlie reviewed his goals daily.

As with other recommendations Charlie made to me in the early years, I didn't do it right away. Although in theory what he said made sense, in reality it didn't. I felt I was too busy or just needed evidence what he was telling me would work.

The fact is, the longer I knew Charlie, the more I knew what he suggested worked. It just did. Goal setting really worked then and to this day continues to do so.

When Charlie first recommended I set and write down

goals I would tell him, "I may do what you tell me, but it may take two or three years before I do them." Charlie would often smile, gently shake his head and let me know that some things were mandatory for success. Looking back, what I realize is that at the time it may just not have been that important or I was so caught up in other things that it didn't seem like the right time to do something.

Even though the concept of goal setting took a while for me to grasp, once I did, the difference in my ability to achieve the outcomes I desired was amazing. Initially I dabbled in the process. Over time, as with virtually every other component of my success, it became very systemized.

It was in the late 1980's that Charlie really pinned me down to do goal setting in a more systemized fashion. In some respects, it was an even more systemized process than I do today. Maybe his age was creating urgency, but this time he was more insistent than he had been.

He said, "Joe, if you want what you say you do, you have to set goals. It's not that difficult and the results will amaze you. Get a blank book. On each page write down your goals in a specific category and date it."

Not only was I to write my goals down, I was to review them morning and night. He had me write my primary goals on a 3 x 5 card to make the review time more targeted. Like other things, I just felt I was too busy, but Charlie would occasionally ask me if I was staying on track with the process. Knowing how important this was to Charlie, I agreed I would give it an honest effort for a specific period of time. This kept me on track with the process.

I don't know if it was the goal setting or all the other factors combined, but amazing events began to happen when I focused on the process of goal setting the way Charlie taught me. I was able to manifest what I wanted a lot quicker and clearer than ever before. Business was booming, my marriage was doing wonderfully, I was becoming very fit and my finances were great.

Charlie not only taught me to set and regularly review my goals, but also to review them every year. It's a kind of check and balance method. Just as a business cannot run efficiently without knowing key bits of information, it is the same with our life.

To know where we are and where we are going, we need to take stock. The first of the year has traditionally been a time to do this. Like me in the early years, many people view this type of process as a time for making resolutions they are not really serious about keeping. Sure, the initial intention may be sincere, but the proof is in how long someone sticks with it.

The goal setting process Charlie shared with me goes beyond a haphazard resolution or one that is simply for amusement; it lays the foundation for success so many people crave.

Today, the process is a part of my success strategy. I wouldn't dream of not using it. The process of a yearly review is one that I have grown to anticipate with great excitement. It allows me the opportunity to reflect on what I have accomplished over the previous year and what is possible in the coming year.

My first serious attempt at setting goals and writing them down was New Year's of 1988 or 1989. The process included some vague goals, but they were goals nonetheless:

1. Personal Growth through reading Books and Tapes
2. Physical Fitness

3. Religion or Spirituality
4. Personal Savings of Money
5. Family Relations
6. Developing Peace of Mind
7. Increasing My Earnings
8. Increasing Quality and Growth of My Office
9. Becoming a Better Manager and a Better Leader
10. Financial Independence
11. Public Speaking

As with most processes, the more I studied goal setting, the more I realized the need to be extremely specific. Each year since that time, without fail, I review my previous goals, evaluate where I am in comparison to where I want to be, refine my current goals and set new ones. I am now much more specific about what I want. For example, in the beginning I might write down, "Read personal growth books." Now I will write, "Read personal development books for 30 to 60 minutes a day."

My goal setting process begins within the first week of the New Year. I have my goal journal in front of me and I review my goals from the previous year. I determine whether I have met my goal, if I need to lessen or heighten the requirement of the goal or eliminate it all together. If I met the goal, do I need to change it?

The journal allows you to see your progression in specific areas each year. Take goals on physical fitness, for example. When your goals are clearly written, you can't deny whether or not you achieved your outcome. If you didn't, you could enhance the goal. In my case, when I reviewed my physical fitness, did I need to increase my running ability or the number of days for working out? By writing my goals down there was no getting around what needed to be done. When you write them down, you hold yourself accountable for your goals.

From the religious or spiritual side, I would look at the commitments I was making to church, retreats or just quiet time. With money, was I saving what I had set down as a goal?

Write your goals in the present tense and attach a feeling to the outcome of the goal. For example, I used to write, "I will run each week." Now I write, "I am so excited, happy and grateful I am running four miles, four days a week. I feel energized and alive because of this."

Most people have heard the expression, "Be careful what you ask for because you will get it." Something I have written down on more than one occasion is 'patience.' In years past, I built a reputation as someone who could often be described as very impatient, so this was an area in which I wanted to improve.

What I have found is that when I ask for something like patience, life will offer me ways to be patient. For example, I may find myself caught in traffic and now I have the opportunity to be 'patient.'

Life will give us what we request. The challenge for most people is that their requests conflict with each other or what they do ask for is so vague they don't realize when they get it. You always get what you ask for. It goes back to one of the most quoted Bible passages, "Ask and ye shall receive."

Ask yourself, "Are my thoughts or actions moving me closer or farther from my goals?"

When someone says to me, "I'm setting goals, but not getting what I want," I invite them to explore the possibility of their beliefs, thoughts and actions. You see, everything is connected. You might say you want something, but if your overriding belief is that you do not deserve it, that you will have to work too hard, or success is for other people, then you are confusing the issue. You have to be so clear on what you want and you have to believe you can have it.

This is why it is important to write your goals on a 3 x 5 inch card that you can carry with you. This allows you to keep your focus on what you do want and not what you don't want.

Today my goals relate to business, personal, physical, spiritual, mental, emotional, financial, and I even have public speaking and writing goals. They are written down in an extremely systemized way and I attach feeling to each of the goals. "*I'm so excited, happy and grateful that now...*"

I have gone as far as laminating the card that I carry around with me. Sometimes I don't even have to read the goals; I can simply touch the card and immediately have a sense of what is there and have a reminder on a regular basis.

At night when I undress, I take my goals card out of my pocket and put it on my bedside table. Now I have a reminder. In the morning, it is one of the first things I am aware of. As you can see, my goals are constantly with me and I can tell you beyond a shadow of a doubt it works.

When I first began the process of goal setting, even before fully adopting Charlie's method, I was setting goals in a very un-systemized way. I would simply repeat in my head the goals I wanted, but I wasn't consistently writing them down. Sure, I would write goals down at different times and different places, but never had them in book form where each goal had a page, each page had a date, and I could see the progression of my goal.

After Charlie repeatedly told me I should be writing them down, I finally started applying his method very deliberately. Once I took his method to heart, I liked the idea of being able to see whether I was achieving or not achieving my goals; of working towards or away from them.

Many doubt the power of writing their goals down and reviewing them on a regular basis. Writing your goals and reading them on a daily basis supports the notion that 'you become what you think about.' If each day you read your financial goals, your conscious and subconscious minds are set into motion moving you closer to what you want. If you've written down your fitness goals, by reviewing them it becomes difficult not to get excited about achieving them.

You have to want to achieve your goals more than you don't want to achieve them. That is why you have to put emotion and feeling into the process. Otherwise, you have no energy invested into the outcome.

I repeatedly tell those I mentor and those who attend my presentations that when you make goals, you are making commitments. If you lie once to yourself about your commitments, the next lie is easier, and then it is no longer a commitment. Then you find yourself justifying why you are not achieving your dreams or you get into the habit of blaming outside circumstances for why life has turned out the way it has. Your goals have to become a commitment. By repeating them and saying you are going to accomplish these goals, it forces you to at least be working towards them.

Success is about our thoughts and beliefs, but it is also about discipline. Successful people are willing to do what unsuccessful people aren't. Unsuccessful people often want what successful people have but they let their doubts take over or they are not willing to put the time and effort into achieving what they say they want. Worse yet, they may want success without any effort.

I once heard a saying that what we do in private we will be rewarded for in public. So it is with our goals. What you are willing to do privately to achieve your goals you will be rewarded for publicly. Discipline yourself in your day-to-day activities in order to reap the benefits and enjoy a life filled with abundance, joy and happiness.

Charlie's words continue to echo in my mind: "You can have anything in life you want if you want it badly enough and are willing to pay the price." Part of the price to pay is determine what you want, write it down, review it morning and night, take the action, adjust the action as needed, evaluate and move forward.

It's important that your goals be aligned with your values. Be careful not to let others steer you away from what you really want to do. If I had listened to my guidance counselor when I was in eleventh grade, I would never have pursued my dream of being a dentist. I can't imagine what my life would have been like had I given in to someone else's doubts.

To achieve many of your goals, there will be work and often what can be considered sacrifice involved. On the other hand, can you imagine what life would be like if you never attempted to go after what you wanted?

Many years ago, one of my goals was to live in a nice house. We didn't have a lot of money at the time, but I knew I wanted a really nice home. When we bought one home, it was a huge stretch. I can remember the real estate agent calling me telling me our bid was accepted. I sat down on the couch with a heavy sigh. Anne looked at me and said, "What's the matter?" I must have looked like I saw a ghost because she said I looked like I was going to pass out. I was achieving the goal I had set my heart on and now I was dealing with the emotions that came with that success and also the fear of the action.

It is one thing to have goals, another to work for the goals and yet another to achieve them. Most goals will take some kind of effort. I knew enough at this time to know the money would show up, it always does, but I also knew there would be effort I needed to put into manifesting the money.

I have also come to realize there is a certain amount of risk that we must take to achieve our goals. I'm somewhat of a calculative risk-taker. I wouldn't be where I am if I wasn't. In spite of a few huge risks I have taken in my life, I always ask myself, "What's the worst that can happen if this doesn't work?" In order to go beyond where you are, you have to stretch.

I don't know about you, but I have a guiding force that helps me walk through any fear. I call him the "little man" inside. The "little man" inside can be called the subconscious or other self.

The more in balance I am, the more in touch with my spiritual side, and the more I realize I have a purpose to fulfill, the clearer the voice of the "little man" becomes.

Another method or tool that will help with achieving your goals is to get involved in a mastermind group. I cannot even begin to convey the benefits and power behind masterminding. I have been involved in several mastermind groups over the years.

The concept of the mastermind group can be traced back to Napoleon Hill in the early 1900's. Many people were introduced to the whole idea of masterminding in his classic book, *Think and Grow Rich*.

He wrote that the mastermind principle is "the coordination of knowledge and effort of two or more people, who work toward a definite purpose, in the spirit of harmony." He explained that, "No two minds ever come together without thereby creating a third, invisible, intangible force, which may be likened to a third mind."

One of the first groups I became involved in was with a group of dentists. There were probably five or six dentists from different dental offices. We would meet with a specific topic, mostly sales or case presentation related. We would role-play our dialogue with both new and existing patient sales calls or Sales Presentations. Using scripts and slides, we would practice until our presentations felt seamless and natural.

Although I understood a mastermind group to be one in which each person would share the role of leader, I was generally the facilitator of the group, usually because the meetings would be held at my office and the other members looked to me to facilitate. What I loved about this first experience was the group energy and being able to share and teach what I knew. I believe it was the unfolding of one of many of my goals. Even years ago I loved sharing with other dentists the systems that were helping me to become a successful dentist and have a successful business. It was also a precursor to what I now do quite frequently; teach others success principles and business building strategies.

It has been said that when you teach, you learn. Through the experience of interacting with this mastermind group, the more I had to prepare to teach what I knew, the better it became ingrained in what I was doing.

Throughout history, some of the great minds of our time have been involved in what could be considered mastermind groups. Through his association with Thomas Edison, Harvey Firestone, and other creative minds, Henry Ford added his own brainpower to the intelligence, experience, knowledge, and spiritual forces of these great men.

Thomas Edison not only had Henry Ford as a mastermind partner, he would also mastermind with many other people. Andrew Carnegie pulled together a team of power thinkers to build the world's greatest steel manufacturing company of its time.

In recent times, Jack Canfield has touted the power of a mastermind group. He says, "We all know that two heads are better than one when it comes to solving a problem or creating a result. So imagine having a permanent group of five or six people who meet every week for the purpose of problem solving, brainstorming, networking, encouraging and motivating each other! Participating in a mastermind group has been critical to me. I can't imagine achieving all I have without one, and it certainly made my goals happen much faster."

Many experts have taught and written about the importance of setting goals and mastermind groups. The book *Think and Grow Rich* by Napoleon Hill was one of the first I read on the subject of mastermind groups. To this day, I still read it because his information works.

Having clear direction is vital to achieving your goals. Not having direction is like trying to take a trip with no plan or map. If you're going to get to Florida, you don't just get in the car and start driving: you need a roadmap, a good car, and all of the necessary supplies to get there. Too many people live their life as if they are getting in the car, beginning to drive with no plan, and hoping to get somewhere. When they live in this way, they either never get there or if they do, they don't know when they have arrived and they keep searching aimlessly.

If you are ready to see how powerful having direction is, chart your future. To begin all you have to do is get an index card and write down a few specific things you want. Pick something for a business or a financial goal, a family goal, a physical goal, a mental/spiritual goal, and any other specific goal you desire. Laminate the card and carry it with you at all times. Read your card every morning and evening.

Try this for a minimum of 30 days and watch what happens. From there, consider forming a mastermind group. Then consider going deeper and deeper into the study of goal setting and gaining direction in your life.

Between goal setting and masterminding, you can achieve great things. As with anything, the more you put into it, the more you will get out of it. It's simply a matter of how much you want something.

Goals are essential for both business and personal success. Most people do not set goals and their level of success and happiness reflect this. Others randomly set personal or professional goals and only achieve partial success.

In order to achieve *TOTAL SUCCESS*, it is essential to set both personal and professional goals on a consistent basis. We'll begin by talking about achieving business success before moving into the area of achieving personal success. A formula for obtaining business success is what I call *The Success Triangle™*. *The Success Triangle™* has been a roadmap for success in my business life and it can be in yours too.

DIRECTION, CLARITY AND VISION
SUCCESS SUMMARY

1. Goal setting is a cornerstone for achievement.
2. Write down and review your goals twice daily – in the morning and at night.
3. Write your goals in the present tense.
4. Write your major goals or a summary of your goals on a 3x5 card and carry it in your pocket.
5. Have goals for all facets of your life: Business/ Financial, Personal, Physical/Health, and Spiritual.
6. Your goals require a commitment and discipline to accomplish them.
7. Review your goals at least once a year.
8. Your goals should be aligned with your values.
9. Mastermind groups can be a help in accomplishing your goals.
10. Goals are essential for both business success and personal success.
11. You can have anything in life if you want it badly enough and are willing to pay the price.

CHAPTER 4

The Success Triangle™

In the next few chapters, I will be sharing with you what has helped me to be successful in my practice. I currently operate a multimillion-dollar dental practice. My income is in the top 3% of dentists in the nation. This did not happen by accident. We followed certain systems and principles in order to achieve this success.

Throughout my 30 plus years in business, I've come to recognize that every business, especially service-oriented businesses, harbor certain needs. Every business needs quality products or services, a well thought through marketing plan and a prescribed way of interacting with potential and existing customers. When these needs are left to chance, most businesses will close their doors, the owners ending their career in a state of overwhelm and exhaustion wondering what happened to their dream.

My desire for a successful business did not manifest by chance, but rather by using a systematic approach to addressing the needs of my business. Nothing is left to chance in my business. Chance is a fickle business partner and success thrives on a system that can be duplicated and repeated. Combine a systematic approach with thoughts, beliefs, feelings and actions, and you become a magnet for business success.

It's amazing how many people don't realize that being a successful dentist goes far beyond being competent in dentistry. A major factor in dentistry success is how good a businessperson you are. As in any company, there are aspects of running a business that all contribute to the level of success you will enjoy. In order to have a successful business, you have to have a solid foundation. The types of systems you have in place support that foundation. Without a strong foundation, success is fleeting at best. Without systems, you will waste precious time, money and energy.

I didn't always understand the importance of foundations and systems. However, when I did determine how important this was to success, I began a quest for knowledge that I continue to this day.

I wanted to be known as a dentist who really cared about my patients. With this in mind, I realized achieving this outcome would require more than just skill; it would require generating the kinds of revenues that allowed me to create an experience for my customers. An experience they would be hard pressed to find elsewhere.

In every business, especially service-oriented businesses, there are certain needs. As I evaluated the main needs of our business, I recognized a business could be very successful using a three-prong approach. This system has been fine-tuned and perfected over a period of decades and is easily demonstrated as *The Success Triangle™*.

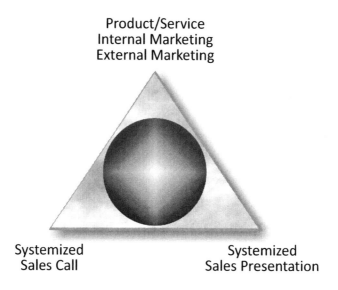

Product/Service
Internal Marketing
External Marketing

Systemized
Sales Call

Systemized
Sales Presentation

This chapter will provide you with an overview of *The Success Triangle™*. Each part will be explored in detail in another chapter.

As in any structure, all reinforcement and strength is built into the foundation, and so it is with *The Success Triangle™*. The triangle consists of your Product, Internal and External Marketing, and your Sales Call and Sales Presentation.

All activities are inter-related and the bottom line relies on understanding that not one of these three areas can stand alone. For example, if your Sales Call or customer meeting (office visit) and/or your Sales Presentation (communications and sales skills) are weak, it impacts dollars spent on Products and Services as well as Internal and External Marketing efforts.

As you look at the triangle, you notice Product/Service is

at the very top. First and foremost, you must have a stellar Product and/or Service. Without a good Product or Service, you may attract customers to your place of business, but they may not turn into repeat customers.

Once you have a stellar Product and/or Service, it is time to focus on Internal Marketing. Internal Marketing is what people see, feel, and touch when they come to your place of business. In essence, Internal Marketing bombards their senses. This includes your place of business; the appearance of your office and how it feels, location and cleanliness. Internal Marketing includes the way customers are handled, what they experience when they enter your office or place of business and what is flooding their senses, right down to the way your employees speak to them. For a remote location business that deals with clients primarily by phone, Internal Marketing would be the experience the person has when they call your company or visit your website. Internal Marketing creates the customer experience.

External Marketing is exactly as it sounds. External Marketing is what you do to encourage people to visit your place of business. It is what you do with "after profit" dollars to attract new customers. It is what you do to position yourself in the marketplace.

There are dozens, even hundreds, of ways to do External Marketing. Before you spend a lot of money on External Marketing, make sure your Product/Service and Internal Marketing are in place and systemized at a high level. Otherwise, you might increase the foot traffic and inquiries to your business and not be able to deliver a good Product or Service or create the kind of experience your customers would be looking for to generate repeat business or referrals.

Your Product/Service, Internal Marketing and External Marketing have an important relationship with each other and on how *The Success Triangle™* works.

For example, let's say you owned a restaurant that had bad food, good customer service, and an average or good facility. You have paid for External Marketing and get people in the door. Is that money wisely spent? I don't think so. Are people going to come back to your restaurant? You do not have a good Product, so probably not.

Here's another scenario. Suppose you have good food, an average or below facility, poor customer service and you are spending money on External Marketing. Do you think that money is wisely spent? I don't think so. Are people going to come back to your restaurant? In this case, they might because they like the food. Customers will sometimes tolerate poor service and a poor facility if the Product or Service is good. The main difference here is that even though they may come back themselves, they won't refer new customers to your business.

Referrals are the essence of a service business. Most service businesses grow on referrals and are supported by External Marketing. External Marketing supports your Internal Marketing and your Product. You need to have a good Product and good Internal Marketing before you spend your dollars on External Marketing.

It is the combination of Product/Service, Internal Marketing and External Marketing that creates a wildly successful business. This doesn't mean you can't do External Marketing while you are getting your systems in place. What you don't want is an imbalance where you are spending lots of money to get people in the door only to deliver a bad Product or poor Service and not having your internal systems in place.

In addition to having a stellar Product and/or Service, Internal and External Marketing are the Systemized Sales Call and the Systemized Sales Presentation. The use of the word 'systemized' is very strategic in my business. I leave nothing to chance. It is not by chance we have built the kind of business I have, it is by design and my systems are a crucial element in my success.

Let's assume we have this perfect world; our Product is great, our Internal Marketing is stellar and we have a beautiful building with skilled employees. Our External Marketing is in place and double or triple the number of people are coming in than we had two or three months ago. We now have people who we have never met or treated coming to our office or business. By having a systemized office visit (or Sales Call) and a Systemized Sales Presentation, we can ensure a higher closure rate. This will maximize the rate of return on the dollars spent on our Product, Internal Marketing and External Marketing.

Systemized Sales Presentations are what we say or do with our customer to help them to say YES to the Products or Services they want or need. Basically, the Systemized Sales Call is our customer encounter. It is the way we deal with our customer: meeting, greeting, selling, and departing from him or her.

Just as there is a relationship between your Product, Internal Marketing and External Marketing to each other, there is also a relationship between the Systemized Sales Presentation and the Systemized Sales Call to each other and to the Product, Internal Marketing and External Marketing.

The base drives the top. If you are effective in your Sales Presentation and your Sales Call, then your dollars spent on Product, Internal Marketing and External Marketing are going to have a greater return.

If you are doing a systemized, effective Sales Call, you will create *trust and confidence*. By building *trust and confidence*, when you do your Systemized Sales Presentation you have a greater chance of the customer saying yes to the Products and Services they want or need.

The purpose of the Sales Call being systemized is to accomplish specific objectives: a warm up, a presentation, a dismissal and a transfer. We will speak about these in detail later, but if you are successful in accomplishing these objectives, you will build trust and confidence in your customer.

This coexistence of the Systemized Sales Call and Systemized Sales Presentation potentiates each other; it makes them more effective. So the greater your skill is in forming the relationship and creating trust and confidence in your Sales Call and the greater your skills in doing a Systemized Sales Presentation, the greater your chance of them saying yes to what you are selling.

When every aspect of *The Success Triangle™* is done in a methodical and systemized way, *success is the natural result*. The base of the triangle — the Systemized Sales Call and the Systemized Sales Presentation — drives the top. It is critical to have systems in place to do both of these effectively.

Systems drive what we do. There is a system associated with each part of *The Success Triangle™*. Success in your business is based on systems. In the book, *The E-Myth Physician*, author Michael Gerber explains the need for systems. "The value of your equity is directly proportional to how well your practice works. And how well your practice works is directly proportional to the effectiveness of your systems you have put into place upon which the operation of your practice depends."

As with any process, taking what is structured and having

your customer experience be as natural and spontaneous as possible takes practice. The process has to be practiced, rehearsed and memorized. As you do it repeatedly, the behavior becomes ingrained and effortless; that's when the unnatural becomes natural. That's the beauty of a system.

I know you may be saying, "I do most or all of these," and you probably do. If your business is where you want it to be, great! Don't change a thing! However, if you want to achieve more success in your business than what you currently have, rethink what you are doing. To do your Sales Call and Sales Presentation the same way all the time requires systems.

In order to develop systems that work, we have to do and learn behaviors that at first seem unnatural to us. As we practice and use these behaviors repetitively, what at first seemed unnatural becomes natural and unrehearsed. You develop what I call unnatural, natural behavior. It becomes a part of who you are; the way you talk, the way you move, and does not seem "canned" or rehearsed. You don't have to think about what you are doing, you just do it.

With *The Success Triangle™*, you not only increase your efficiency, you also increase your team's; the customer experience is enhanced, and ultimately your revenues and profit margins increase. With increased revenues and profit margins, you are in more of a position to create the kind of business you want.

The processes I have developed can be applied to virtually any business. When these processes are implemented, you will grow your business beyond your wildest dreams.

THE SUCCESS TRIANGLE™
SUCCESS SUMMARY

1. The Product or Service is the most important part of *The Success Triangle™*.

2. A good Product and good Internal Marketing is needed to generate referrals.

3. Most service businesses grow mainly from referrals.

4. An outstanding Product and stellar Internal Marketing are needed prior to extensive External Marketing.

5. There are costs involved with having an outstanding Product and stellar Internal Marketing. This is a requirement — not an option — for success in a service business.

6. The requirement for External Marketing can vary depending on the type of service business.

7. External Marketing dollars come from profit dollars so it is essential to External Market wisely to get a maximum return on your investment.

8. A system or plan for Internal and External Marketing is needed to maximize your return on dollars spent.

9. Your Systemized Sales Call and Systemized Sales Presentation support your Product, Internal Marketing and External Marketing. The better you are with these two areas, the more Product is sold thus maximizing your dollars spent on Product, Internal Marketing and External Marketing.

10. The Systemized Sales Call links to the Systemized Sales Presentation and vice versa with both

supporting the top of *The Success Triangle™*. Both areas are system driven and potentiates, or has a synergistic effect, on each other.

11. A Systemized Sales Call creates trust and confidence, which leads to higher sales acceptance.

12. A Systemized Sales Presentation based on principles of respect leads to higher sales acceptance. It all connects with the Systemized Sales Call (SSC) and Systemized Sales Presentation (SSP).

13. Success is exponential.
   - If you are a 5 in a SSC and a 5 in a SSP, then 5 + 5=10
   - If you are a 8 in a SSC and a 5 in a SSP, then 8 + 5=16
   - If you are a 8 in a SSC and a 8 in a SSP, then 8 + 8=22
   - If you are a 9 in a SSC and a 9 in a SSP, then 9 + 9=30

   This shows the potentiation and synergistic effect of these two skills. You reach a point where 1 + 1 no longer equals 2.

14. The base drives the dollars spent on the top of the triangle, the money spent on Product, Internal Marketing and External Marketing.

Now you have a great overview of the power of *The Success Triangle™*. There is a very specific order of developing your business systems based on *The Success Triangle™* which we will explore in more detail in the following chapters. You will also see a very definite relationship between your Product or Service, Internal Marketing and External Marketing in order to achieve success in your business.

Chapter 5

Developing Your Business Systems

Product/Service Excellence

At the top of *The Success Triangle™* you find Product/Service, Internal and External Marketing. Before you can have a successful business, you first have to have a great Product. If you don't, you are training people to promote something that is of poor quality. You won't go anywhere with a bad Product.

Product and Service development is an ongoing process. It requires keeping up on your industry, what your customers need and want, specialized training and continuing education.

Associating with other professionals who are more successful than you can help tremendously to increase your

Product and Service offerings and quality of work. It will also force you to raise your own standards.

You can acquire training on just about any topic when it comes to learning more about your Product or Service. The desire to offer the best is something that goes beyond reading a book, taking a course, or getting a certification. It comes from within. It comes from the way you think. When you have thoughts of excellence, you will do whatever it takes to become very knowledgeable about your industry, your Products and Services and your customer's needs and wants.

In dentistry, there are several resources where my team and I can obtain further information: the Las Vegas Institute of Advanced Dental Studies, national training centers, trade journals, private seminars, vendor courses, and online courses to name just a few.

In your industry, finding the resources to improve your Product quality and Product knowledge is as close as your computer keyboard. How much you choose to invest is up to you. If you want to be the best, you must invest in the best.

INTERNAL MARKETING

Once you have your Product and Service at a level you are proud of, it is time to focus on your Internal Marketing. Internal Marketing is what people see, feel, and touch when they come to your place of business. In essence, Internal Marketing is what your customer senses; it is the customer experience.

Internal Marketing encompasses the entire customer experience, including the way customers are treated, what they experience when they enter your business, and how they are spoken to by you and your employees. Internal Marketing actually begins with the first phone call made to your business.

Internal Marketing can vary with the size and type of company and the number of employees. We've all been on the receiving end of good Internal Marketing. Nordstrom's is known for their customer friendly return policy as well as their no pressure sales team. Southwest Airlines revolutionized the flying experience with customer friendly flight crews, low cost fares and an easy, hassle free check-in process.

The cover story in the March 2007 issue of Business Week gives us a glimpse into the Top 25 companies who demonstrate great Internal Marketing! A few of the companies profiled are USSA Insurance, Four Seasons Hotels and Resorts, Cadillac, Edward Jones, UPS, Enterprise Rent-a-Car, Starbucks, Lincoln, Porsche, The Ritz-Carlton, Southwest Airlines, Hertz, FedEx, JW Marriott Hotels and Resorts, T-Mobile, Apple and Lexus.

Each has a unique approach to who their customer is, how they address customer needs and wants, and ultimately how they stand apart in the market. These companies understand the power that Internal Marketing has to enhance both the experience and perception of their customers.

A fact often overlooked by many companies is many customers frequent an establishment solely because of their Internal Marketing. Their experience and perception of the business are so positive that they tend to ignore pricing altogether.

As powerful as Internal Marketing is, it is frequently disregarded or under-appreciated by many businesses. It is rare that a company can neglect Internal Marketing without a negative impact on their success.

This was not an immediate revelation for me. In fact, if we were to benchmark my practice even 15 years ago against other dental practices, we were head and shoulders above the rest. Yet if we benchmarked ourselves against high-end businesses or high-end customer service establishments like the Four Seasons Hotel or the Ritz-Carlton, we were definitely not up to speed.

The goal for my practice was to create an experience I'd found as a guest at a five-star establishment. I wanted to create an experience that lasted long after the patient left our office. I wanted our Internal Marketing to be so exceptional that when we did our case presentation, which in other industries is the Sales Presentation, the only answer our patient could muster would be a YES! This did not happen overnight nor did we do this alone. If we were going to systemize the patient experience during an office visit, we were going to need some help.

Although we'd been conducting in-house training for our team since 1985 in order to have above average customer service, it was around 2000 that I decided to ramp up our training so every patient's wants and desires were addressed. This was a huge shift for us because by dental office standards, we were already good, but we wanted to move to exceptional. We were beginning to External Market for cosmetic dentistry. I decided that before we spent money to get people in the door, we needed to sharpen our Internal Marketing. Up until this point, we had been focusing on a need-based dentistry. We were a dental practice that took a historical approach to dentistry, which meant waiting for the patient to need our services. Now that we were in cosmetic dentistry, our market shifted from need-based dentistry to want-based dentistry. If we were to attract want-based customers, we needed a better customer experience.

I was intent on creating a reputation as something other than a run-of-the-mill general dentist. I wanted to be known as an outstanding cosmetic dental practice and that was a very different image.

To do this we contracted the services of one of the industries leading experts, Bob Maccario. Bob is recognized as the Dental Concierge and is in high demand for training and consulting because of his expertise. In your industry, you are likely to find experts who are as recognized as Bob is in the dental industry.

Bob taught us the importance of patient interaction and how each person's specific personality type dictates their style of communication. He indoctrinated us in the DiSC® Classic system. This gave us a method to understand our patients and ourselves in a powerful new way. Adopting the DiSC® Classic system into our practice was a major turning point for our success. (You will learn in detail about profiling your customers with DiSC® Classic and its importance and impact on your business in an upcoming chapter.)

Although the investment for Bob was high, I knew this was something we had to do. As with any other time I stretched myself, if I wanted to go to the next level, I had to be willing to feel some discomfort to achieve my goals.

I have to laugh now when I think about all the people who tried to discourage me from investing in training. Some of my peers said I was crazy for spending so much on Bob. Usually, they were the people who had average businesses and average lives. I wanted more than average!

Another distinction between successful people and those who will never achieve a high level of success is we view training as an investment rather than simply spending money.

DiSC® is a registered trademark of Inscape Publishing, Inc.

I'm a big believer in professional development and continuing education; my office has always been actively involved in professional development and team training. We wouldn't be where we are today without it.

An essential part of what Bob taught was about creating an experience for the patient/customer. Internal Marketing and customer care are a big part of the experience.

I firmly believe outstanding Internal Marketing is driven by committed and talented team members. There are several things we have done, and continue to do, that have allowed us to enjoy overall business success.

Bob taught us the importance of what we call "the people working in the business." We don't use the word "staff" in our office; we jokingly say *Staff is an infection.* We are all members of a team and our work environment is designed to bring out the best in us.

Before we could be effective with our Internal Marketing, it was essential to know what kind of business we wanted to create. A few considerations were (and continue to be):

- Who do we want to do business with?
- What experience do we want to create for our customers?
- When people talk to others about our practice, what will they say?

Once we became very clear on who we are, what we offer and who we want to do business with, we were able to be very systematic and targeted in our approach to Internal Marketing.

With a new set of goals in sight, we took a good dental practice and turned it into a business that exceeded our wildest dreams. We took every component of serving the customer and systemized it. From the moment a potential patient calls, we have a script and a methodical approach to interacting with our new patient.

Our Internal Marketing includes understanding the customer's perspective right down to how they are greeted and how they feel in our building. We maintain a facility that is spotless, attractive and impressive. Our restrooms are beautiful and luxurious. Our décor is inviting and stylish. The front desk team has a wonderful demeanor, which includes the sound of their voices; they're mild-mannered and soft-spoken.

Systemizing was a huge turning point for our business. Now our entire team was on the same page and the customer experience was stellar. We were no longer an average practice. We were noticing more and more that we were attracting a higher level of customer. We were attracting customers who were looking for more than simply getting dental work done; they also wanted a stellar experience when they came to our office.

We didn't make all the changes overnight. It was and continues to be a process. The first place we started was to identify specific team members to deal with new patients.

Because it is part of *The Success Triangle™* system, the new patient interaction is handled in the same manner all the time; it's not hit or miss. When a new patient calls our office, we ask how they found us, what are they coming in for, and what concerns they have. We create a relationship on the phone long before they enter our office.

Our office conducts business much differently than most dental practices. For instance, if our receptionist handles a phone call and there's a question or concern, she directs the patient to the person who is responsible for that particular area of concern. We do not have our receptionist doing double and triple duty as you see in many practices. Her job is to answer the phone, take care of the patient's request and function as a greeter. She is the patient's first point of contact.

In other dental practices, anyone who is available might be tasked with patient scheduling. Even though we're a multiple-provider office, each dentist has a scheduling coordinator and two dental assistants; they all function as a team for that particular dentist. When a patient comes in and walks to the front desk, they are greeted and asked about their unique circumstances. They are then directed to the coordinator who works with their specific dentist.

Our patients know their coordinator and they know they will talk to the same coordinator on future visits. We create a sense of routine for the patient, which in turn develops trust and an experience of quality.

We work hard to make our customer's experience pleasant and memorable from the first moment of contact. We want everyone who calls our office to have a good experience on the phone and everyone who walks in our office to be pleasantly surprised by the décor and decorum. We have flowers throughout the office. We offer different kinds of snacks to our customers on different days. We have pretzel days, pastry days and doughnut days in our office. We offer several beverages and we make the beverage for the customer. Upon their request, we serve coffee, juice or water.

I know there are other businesses, including other dental offices that offer a "perk" such as beverages. Having the beverage is only part of the experience. Serving it to a customer is the distinction of the experience. It is the same with how we gather personal information.

Unlike countless other businesses, including other dental and medical offices, our customers are never given a clipboard and told, "Fill this paperwork out." We sit down with the person in a private area and help them complete the paperwork. We provide these services from a customer care and Internal Marketing standpoint. We want our customers to be comfortable and make their time in our facility easy, predictable and memorable.

There is no question about it: I want to stand out from the rest. We have worked hard at not being known as an ordinary practice and we want all of our customers to know it. To excel in these areas, one must be conscious and intentional in serving their customers and very deliberate in their Internal Marketing.

Cosmetic dentistry is a want-based product, which requires a higher level of customer service and Internal Marketing. The goal was no longer just to get the patient in the door. The goal was to get them in, have them stay, accept treatment, spend dollars and refer other customers. Getting them in the door was just the beginning.

As you think of your own business, what is the experience your customer has when they walk into or drive by your building? Does it support the message, "When you come to us, you know we care?"

EXTERNAL MARKETING

Although External Marketing is an essential aspect of business success, many lose sight of the fact that you must first have your Product development and Internal Marketing in order to optimize External Marketing investments since External Marketing dollars come from profit dollars. Before investing in

External Marketing, it is important to understand your industry's market trends. Pay attention to what your customer's current needs are and adjust your Product or Service accordingly.

External Marketing should be viewed as an investment, not an expense. The reason it is often seen as an expense is businesses are not strategic in their approach to their External Marketing.

When done right and as a part of the whole system, you can obtain incredible results through creative and systematic approaches to your External Marketing. The fact is, if you have a good Product and good Internal Marketing with no External Marketing, you could probably get by. But if you want to be a success at attracting more customers or more high end-customers, you need to engage in External Marketing. A note of caution: Do not begin your External Marketing until the quality of your Product and your Internal Marketing are solid!

Many businesses have not educated themselves on what marketing is and is not. Many think advertising in and of itself is marketing. Advertising is just one aspect of marketing. Traditional methods of External Marketing can include direct marketing, newsletters, newspapers, magazines, billboards, broadcast media, yellow pages, and door hangers. With the onslaught of technology, you can use various other forms of External Marketing including websites, blogs and email promotions.

In the dental industry, many dentists feel either they don't need to advertise, or if they do, they think running a yellow page ad is all they need. As mentioned previously, if your Internal Marketing systems are not in place, you will be wasting your External Marketing dollars. Rather than haphazardly running advertisements, develop a system where one part of your

External Marketing supports another.

Over the years, I made conscious choices in how much I would grow my practice. What started out as a two chair, two dentist practice became an 18 chair, 50-plus employee, seven dentist practice. This did not happen overnight, nor is my type of practice for everyone.

I developed my Products and Services to a level beyond what most practices were doing and my Internal Marketing was beyond compare. From there, I attempted to do some External Marketing. Initially, I did much the same marketing as other dentists did.

Then something shifted. I went from advertising and marketing to value added marketing. Based on a few training courses I took, hiring some of the best consultants in the industry and realizing I now needed to be a resource before a vendor, I completely shifted how and when I was advertising *and* my overall marketing strategies.

Granted, the process of running a few ads in the local paper and in the yellow pages might have been easier, but as with everything that has set me apart, I didn't want easier, I wanted distinction. Distinction in the marketplace, in my customer's mind, in the way I ran my business, and in the Services and Products I offer.

Knowing I needed to understand what marketing was and was not, I proceeded to educate myself on what was available. With no marketing training in dental school, I must admit, some of what I learned worked, but most of the information I had was very misguided and a complete waste of time, money and effort. What I came to realize very early on was the stronger my Internal Marketing, the higher return I received on my External Marketing.

Like most dentists, I ran yellow page ads, did some print advertising and direct mail pieces. The challenge with the advertising was there was no way for the consumer to differentiate between me and every other practice that ran an ad. When websites became popular, I jumped on board with that.

As with everything else, I wanted the image I projected to be outstanding, so I hired a very skilled web designer. I came to realize that the website in and of itself may not get me any business, but if someone is "checking out" my practice, they may look at my site and based on what they find, decide I am credible. I have had this happen more than once. When a patient is asked where they heard about us, often they will say, "I saw your magazine ad and then checked out your website. Your site was so nice I knew you were someone I would want to work on my teeth." Go figure. To me that may not be a reason to choose a dentist, but obviously to some patients it is.

It is the same in your industry. You have to know how and why your customers make decisions. What makes your business credible in your customer's eyes?

When I decided it was time to become extremely targeted with my External Marketing, I experienced a number of very interesting events. I was selected as the dentist of choice for the Philadelphia NBA Sixers Dancers. It was also around that time I decided to run some very high-end magazine advertisements. In conjunction with my recognition as the dentist of choice for the Sixers Dancers, I also decided to participate in a radio campaign. The print ads included a picture of me with the Sixers Dancers with the caption: "Congratulations to Dr. Joe Capista of Williamsburg Dental, Selected as the Preferred Dentist of Choice for the Seventy Sixer Dancers."

In the local market, my advertising was raising my visibility exponentially. It got to the point that almost everywhere I went, people would comment on one of my ads.

Keep in mind I took a systematic approach to how I conducted my External Marketing efforts. I was consciously investing in an overall marketing strategy, something many businesses fail to do. Instead, they take an approach similar to the one I did early on - haphazard.

One of the most important details I have learned about External Marketing is the need to be a resource before I am a vendor. Become the expert in your industry that everyone goes to when they have questions. Simply put, when I educate my market rather than simply try to sell a Product to them, I will have a greater result.

It was around 2004 when I had another turning point in my business. I had just begun a new type of marketing: hosting information seminars. The purpose of these public seminars was to inform participants about their choices in dentistry with a very strong emphasis on cosmetic dentistry.

As much as the Dental Concierge educated me on Internal Marketing, my marketing advisor, Kathleen Gage, gave me incredible insights into a very unique way to optimize my seminar approach.

When I first met Kathleen at a training seminar hosted by Becden Dental Laboratory in Draper, Utah, I had already hosted a couple of my own sessions. Although they were successful, Kathleen showed me how to gain an even greater benefit from them. I began to understand fully that by offering information seminars coupled with my other marketing efforts, I was able to literally gain a corner on my market.

The whole idea behind the seminars was to inform my

current and potential customers what dentistry had to offer in the past, present and future. Since I had a high percentage of customers seeking cosmetic solutions, it made perfect sense to use a very soft approach when introducing these options.

It is important to remember that whatever you invest in External Marketing must be fully supported by a high quality Product and/or Service as well as a great Internal Marketing program. Your greatest success is not going to come from External Marketing. It comes from the quality, experience and perceived value of your customers.

This is a big problem in many businesses; they are not deliberate in their efforts. They are flying by the seat of their pants hoping for the best. Most businesses have a Product and some type of Internal Marketing. More often than not, their Internal Marketing is poor to average. Then they wonder why they are not achieving the revenue levels they desire.

The same happens when you have poor or average External Marketing. In the absence of well thought-out Internal and External Marketing strategies, businesses lose both money and customers.

It is when you take a holistic approach to your business you will experience business success.

BUSINESS SUCCESS
THE SUCCESS TRIANGLE™ SUMMARY

By now, I am sure you have found great value in the information about the primary aspects of *The Success Triangle™*. I have shown how important each element is. Two important elements of *The Success Triangle™* are the Systemized Sales Call and the Systemized Sales Presentation. In Chapters 6 and 7, you will learn in detail how to optimize these components of the full system.

As with the other aspects of *The Success Triangle™*, both the Sales Call and Sales Presentation must be well planned to create an experience like none other.

In the Sales Call, you want to create an above-average relationship, value for your Product or Service, a five-star experience, and trust and confidence in the customer's mind.

In your Sales Presentation, you want to have a system where your customer has a greater chance of saying YES to your Product or Service. Ultimately, you want your sales acceptance to be high as well as your customer satisfaction.

As previously mentioned, a huge factor in successfully utilizing *The Success Triangle™* system is in knowing who we want to do business with and why we want to do business with them. Unfortunately, many business owners, salespeople and entrepreneurs have given little if any thought to whom they ideally want to do business with. Their mentality is that everyone is their market. When everyone is your market, your focus is blurred and your marketing efforts are minimized. Selecting your ideal customers requires fine-tuning your goals and defining your market.

I defined my market by recognizing there are certain services I like to provide as a dentist. I like doing cosmetic dentistry. I do not like doing dentures or braces. Because of this, I do not market to senior citizens regarding dentures or parents about braces. I market to men and women between the ages of 45 to 60 who are interested in aesthetics. I market to baby-boomers who have expendable income and want to look their best.

Baby boomers want to feel good and they like to spend money on themselves. That's the market that I'm going after. The baby boomer generation is my target market. I'm very clear on this fact. Because I have so much clarity, I can offer stellar Products, set up my Internal Marketing systems to optimize my customer's experience and market in a way that attracts the people who are a great fit for my services.

I didn't always know this. My revenues and minimal professional satisfaction reflected my lack of focus. However, by having extensive training, great mentors and digging deep into who I am as a dentist, business owner and as a person, I have been able to achieve amazing results. Best of all, I have a much higher client satisfaction and appreciation rating.

Here's an example of why knowing your market is so important. Let's take Internal Marketing. If I had a restaurant and I wanted to market to baby boomers, I'd have an art-deco facility with a neat looking bar, high-end food and a sophisticated menu. My food would be more sophisticated than a family restaurant would likely offer. I would have a very skilled chef preparing the meals.

With my External Marketing, I'm not going to advertise in the *Town Talk*, the local throw-away paper. I'm going to be in a high-end publication like *Philadelphia Magazine*. I'm going to show pictures of my establishment with current customers who resonate with our potential customer population. That's basic marketing; target the people you want. It is very important to understand your Product, your market, and what it ultimately takes to get to a YES at the close. As simple as it sounds, many businesses fail at *The Success Triangle™*.

This is a BIG PICTURE conversation. Each part of *The Success Triangle™* is important individually, but when executed together, there is a synergy and potentiation of each area. To thrive, our view must include what it takes to compliment and strengthen all aspects of our business.

Before spending dollars on External Marketing to attract new patients, we have to be conscious of the way we handle our current customers in a Sales Call, the way we deliver our Sales Presentation and the quality of Product we're providing. We must consider all aspects of the triangle before we spend significant dollars on External Marketing.

In the early stages of defining *The Success Triangle™*, we worked to systemize the customer experience or Sales Call. This meant we had to systemize the way we interacted with our customer. I quickly found that Internal Marketing and a strong Sales Call (in our case, the Office Visit) went hand in hand creating comfort and certainty on the patient's behalf. The combination of the two increased our closure rate when we did our Systemized Sales Call and Sales Presentation, which in turn supported our External Marketing Dollars.

To access a printable version of *The Success Triangle™*, visit www.TheSuccessTriangle.com.

PRODUCT / SERVICE DEVELOPMENT
SUCCESS SUMMARY

1. A good or above average Product and/or Service are essential for success.
2. Do not try to market a poor or even average Product.
3. Be an expert at what you do.
4. If you are not the best in your industry, be the best you can be.

5. Always ask yourself, "Is this the best Product or Service I can offer?"
6. Offer the best Product or Service to all of your customers.
7. Let them decide if they do not want the best.
8. To have the best Product or Service requires ongoing improvement of your skills.
9. Your Product or Service is a reflection of you.
10. Be proud of your Product and/or Service.

INTERNAL MARKETING SUCCESS SUMMARY

1. Your appearance is part of Internal Marketing. Always be well groomed and dress the way your customer expects you to. Look at yourself or have someone critique your appearance.
2. The appearance of your employees is part of your Internal Marketing. If your employees have customer contact, they should dress appropriately and the way your customer expects. Some employees need to be educated about the importance of grooming.
3. The appearance of your facility, both inside and out, is part of Internal Marketing. Look at your facility as if you were the customer. What works well? What needs to be changed? Do this on a regular basis.
4. The manner in which your employees speak is part of customer service. Start with good grammar and then train employees on phone skills and in personal dialogues.
5. Send handwritten Thank You notes for referrals and

to new customers. Emails do not work here. In a high-tech world, high-touch is more important. Use nice, custom-printed Thank You note stationary.

6. Follow up a service with a phone call. Not new, but a sincere phone call lets the customer know you care. Try not to leave messages on answering machines when at all possible.

7. Fill out paperwork for your customer. Do not have your customer fill out forms by themselves. Sit down with them and do the writing. At times it may take longer, but in doing this you will start relationship building with your customer.

8. Have a good logo, stationary and collateral marketing pieces. Do not try to do this yourself — it will usually look like you did! Pay an expert to create a logo and other marketing pieces. Do not take the first example they show you. Be fussy — these materials are a reflection of you and your business!

9. Ask for referrals. Develop a learned dialogue to ask for referrals. It should be short, sincere and not aggressive.

10. Get help from experts. There are many experts out there for Internal Marketing. Find people you like and trust to give you help in this area.

EXTERNAL MARKETING
SUCCESS SUMMARY

1. Understand that advertising is just a piece of your marketing. Get help from experts. Many times an ad

needs to be more about the customer and less about you. An option to a standard ad would be an "advertorial" in newsprint or magazines. These editorial-type ads will give valid information to prospective clients and will define you as an expert in your field.

2. Have a vision. You can get frustrated and waste time and money without a vision. You need to know who you want to attract, the type or level of marketing you want to do, how long you want to do a marketing project, an expected rate of return and how much you want to spend.

3. Budget your spending. If you have a budget, you know you have a specific amount of money put aside verses spending aimlessly. Without a budget, there can be a tendency to limit or stop marketing if you do not see instant results. Having a budget gives you some staying power.

4. Limit External Marketing until you have a good Product or Service and good Internal Marketing. Without a good Product or Service and good Internal Marketing, it is difficult to have a happy customer and therefore you are not effectively spending your money on External Marketing.

5. External Marketing dollars come directly from profit dollars. Use experts and have a marketing plan.

6. Have a website. You not only need a website, you need a good website. Give your customers a place to visit prior to coming into the office.

7. Become a resource before becoming a vendor. Give seminars about your business or Product.

8. Develop sponsorships. This will be my fourth year as "The Cosmetic Dentist for the Sixers Dancers." This sponsorship has been invaluable for creating and validating the perception of an expert. You can develop sponsorship at different levels to gain this exposure. It doesn't have to be a sports team.

9. Develop low and no cost External Marketing. This can be done by giving a talk, presentation or seminar. Another option would be press releases from people with whom you advertise.

10. Track what you do. Know what works. Ask your customers how they found you, etc. Many times, it is not just one External Marketing factor that attracts customers, so see what is working the best. What works can also change from year to year.

Having a stellar Product or Service and systemizing your Internal and External Marketing are what allow you to be fully prepared for opportunity. An essential part of your business opportunity resides in your ability to systemize your approach to the Sales Call. Many people leave this part of their business system to chance. The more systemized your approach to the Sales Call, the more efficient you will become.

Chapter 6

The Systemized Sales Call

Customer interactions are left to chance by most business owners, salespeople and employees. There are hundreds of programs designed to track every customer's whim. Regardless of how diligent you are in using a customer contact program, if you do not use your skills as a communicator and relationship builder, you are missing your full potential for dream-making success.

My first ten plus years in business were the same as it is for many people; just figure out how to run the business. However, once I accomplished that and realized I wanted more than simply a dental practice, I began a quest to become a leader in my field.

As I explained in detail in *The Success Triangle™* chapter, systems are at the root of business success. Every company who made the Top 25 list mentioned in Business Week in March 2007 are proponents of systems.

Taking the idea of systems to a deeper level, over the course of the last 20 years, I've developed a systemized approach to working with our customers that involves a four-stage process. This approach is the result of anticipating our customer's expectations, studying their behaviors during the office visit, and understanding and respecting their communication style. The four stages culminate in a much higher closure rate as well as customers who are fiercely loyal.

I'm a firm believer that systems drive the success of our businesses. The better our systems, the better our business runs. The better the business runs, the less effort required for success. A large part of my goal with my business is to succeed effortlessly! A big part of my goal in writing this book is to show you how systems can increase your success.

My goal of effortless success has not come easily. I've always had an inherent dissatisfaction that prompts me to improve everything I can in my business and my personal life. I can remember many years ago standing at the sink washing my hands while staring into space. Anne knew me well enough by this point in our marriage to know I was deep in thought analyzing something.

"What are you thinking about?" she says tapping me on the shoulder.

Without hesitation I responded, "Oh, we've got to do this better at work, and this isn't up to speed and we're going to work on this..."

She lamented saying, "You're never satisfied. As good as things are, you're just never satisfied."

"You're right, I'm never satisfied," I responded. What I

knew then and I know now is that I'll never be satisfied. I believe that being satisfied is being average. I don't want an average business, I don't want an average relationship, and I don't want an average life. So I never want to be "satisfied."

This doesn't mean I'm not happy, content or pleased with what I'm doing and extremely grateful for what I have; it just means I'm not satisfied with the way things are. I have found there has to be a degree of dissatisfaction in work and life in order to improve. It's hard to improve if you're satisfied with what you have.

As we set out to improve every aspect of the customer experience, we developed an approach in our office we call the Systemized Sales Call. In dentistry, this is also known as the office visit.

Unfortunately, this is where numerous businesses and sales professionals leave their success to chance. In our office, we don't leave anything to chance. Each step has a customized script; nothing is haphazard when dealing with our patients. Our entire team is trained in every aspect of the process and expected to be intentionally systematic every step of the way.

This doesn't mean that we are so systemized we lose our personality. Actually, it is quite the contrary. The more we know and understand the systems, the more we can enjoy the process and really be ourselves. It's like a winning sports team. By the time they get to play the game, they have invested hours and hours of practice, strategic planning, systems and coaching to be the best they can be. They don't leave their success to chance.

And you shouldn't either when it comes to your business.

THE FOUR STAGES OF
THE SYSTEMIZED SALES CALL

There are four stages of a Systemized Sales Call: the Warm-Up, Dialogue, Dismissal and Transfer. You'll notice as you become familiar with each stage that the customer's needs and wants are a priority at every juncture. The terms are practical in nature yet customer driven in outcomes.

The Warm-Up Stage is just as it implies: a time to connect, to get to know one another and create a sense of relationship with our customer. We are very methodical and respectful of this time with our patients and customers. We consider the Warm-Up Stage to be the framework for everything to come. This is the place where we create a relationship that develops trust and confidence. Amazingly, we do this in fairly short order.

The Dialogue Stage in essence is the Sales Presentation. It is what you say about your Product, highlighting the features and benefits, and a time to create value or perceived value for your Product or to resell past purchases. In the Dialogue Stage, you educate your customer so they are able to make an informed decision to buy. Dialogue will be discussed at length in the chapter titled The Sales Presentation.

The Dismissal Stage is a shifting of gears. We went from Warm-Up (relationship building) and Dialogue (discussing Product benefits, features and past purchases) to the Dismissal Stage. The Dismissal Stage occurs when we've completed the Dialogue; the customer has made a decision on Product and Services and I am about to dismiss myself. Before I dismiss myself, I reconnect with the patient on a personal level, reestablishing the relationship and reassuring the customer of their decision to buy.

The Transfer Stage is when we transfer the financial obligations and responsibilities to an experienced team member. Not unlike buying a car, you are greeted by and sold to by a sales professional, but someone else handles the financials. We make every effort to make the transfer smooth, professional and feel like a natural step in the process. In fact, our patients appreciate working the details out with someone who is an expert and well versed in financial options.

The Transfer Stage has been an essential aspect of our system. In many businesses, one person tries to do everything. There are occasions where it is more appropriate and professional for you to not be responsible for handling the paperwork. Having someone who has been trained in answering questions about the details of any financing is the best route to take.

Let's take a look at each stage in greater detail.

WARM-UP

The Warm-Up Stage allows us to connect and build a relationship with our customer. To assist us in the Warm-Up Stage, we've become proficient in using the DiSC® Classic learning tool by Inscape Publishing. My team and I are well versed in the behaviors and characteristics of each style. We have had a great deal of training on how to use this system. We didn't simply read a book about it, we hired a consultant to give us in-depth training.

When I was first introduced to the DiSC® Classic system, I was very excited about what it could do for us. So much, in fact, I paid to have my entire team go through intensive training. The training was one of the best investments we made because we were now in a position to more fully understand, appreciate and respect our customers' communication styles and preferences. To learn more about DiSC® Classic, visit The Success Triangle™ website at www.thesuccesstriangle.com.

Our ability to identify a customer's predominant communication and behavior style gives us insight into both motivations and resistance. We are deeply respectful of our customers and want to be able to communicate in a way that shows we are very connected with them. Please note that the use of DiSC® Classic is to discipline ourselves to communicate in a way that is comfortable for our customers; it is not intended to trick or manipulate them into buying a Product they don't want.

For the new and existing customer, the Warm-Up Stage is not the time we discuss business. It is a time when we focus all of our attention on who they are before we get into why they are here.

This is the time we say, "Tell me a little bit about yourself. How long have you worked at your current job? How many children do you have? Have you lived here a long time? Do you play golf? What does your spouse do? What are your hobbies?"

The questions I ask during the Warm-Up Stage are questions of investigation. I'm searching for who the person is before we talk about what they want.

In the Warm-Up stage, the DiSC® Classic profile is very important. DiSC® Classic describes four different behavioral styles that our customer population falls into. The DiSC® Classic system is based upon Dr. William Marston's model of behaviors and environmental perceptions. Each letter represents a style and each customer will gravitate to one style over another.

Dr. William Marston originally created the DiSC® system. It was researched and updated by Inscape Publishing. The DiSC® model has helped over 35 million people in twenty plus languages over the last 40 years. With that kind of track record, we know it is a solid tool for enhancing our customer's experience.

The DiSC® Classic system identifies four behavior styles: Dominance, Influence, Steadiness, and Conscientious. A description of each style follows.

DOMINANCE (D)

All styles have what can be interpreted as positive and negative traits. D is no exception. On the positive side, highly Dominant individuals are independently minded, motivated to succeed, and generally very effective at getting their own way. On the negative side, they can be short-tempered and even aggressive under certain conditions.

Dominance can be summarized as the factor of control. People with this style prominent in DiSC® Classic focus on the need to achieve and maintain a measure of authority and power over other people and, more generally, the environment in which they live and work. Competitiveness and ambition are also associated with the D profile. People showing a high D will strive to achieve their aims and goals in life against great odds. High D's seem to enjoy challenge and rarely back away from a difficult or risky situation.

High D individuals are not naturally trusting of others - they will seek to attain success on their own merits, without asking for or expecting help or support from those around them. Should a situation arise where the assistance of others is an unavoidable necessity, they will tend to issue orders directly rather than asking for co-operation. High D people can be described as demanding, egocentric, forceful, driving, pushy, determined, ambitious, aggressive, pioneering, and visionary.

INFLUENCE (I)

As you might expect, people with High Influence are gregarious, sociable and often possess well-developed social skills with an incredible urge to meet and talk with other people. The communicative and socially confident style of those with High I tend to be balanced by a rather impulsive and sometimes fun loving approach to life. The urge to relate to and impress those around them can lead to acting in ways that other less socially oriented types find very difficult to understand.

High I's need to interact positively with those around them. Their friendly, open style usually helps them to maintain relationships. The socially active nature of a High I person is often an important factor in bringing other less gregarious styles together.

By their nature, High I's are extremely trusting. Their desire to be open with other people can lead them at times to reveal information or express feelings that others might keep private.

They are often described as magnetic, influencing, convincing, persuasive, warm, trusting, demonstrative, optimistic, and enthusiastic.

STEADINESS (S)

There are a number of strengths linked to the Steadiness

style. People of this kind are patient and sympathetic listeners, with a real interest in the problems and feelings of others. They are particularly capable of fulfilling support roles. They also have a persistent approach with powers of concentration that allow them to work for long periods of time on a task. While others might become bored or distracted, the High S will continue to work until they complete a task. They like to do one task well and then move on to the next project. They are not multitasking oriented.

High S's are resistant to change and prefer a predictable and constant environment. They work best when given clear instructions and a high level of support. Because of this, they avoid conflict or confrontation and will adopt the role of peacemaker.

A very High S can be recognized by their traits of being extremely calm, relaxed, patient, predictable, and deliberate. They are also possessive, deliberate, stable, unemotional, slow moving and resistant to change.

CONSCIENTIOUS (C)

C is the style of structure, detail and fact. Those who are High C's are interested in quality and accuracy. They are similar to highly Dominant individuals in their desire for control over their environment. Unlike D's, they will try to achieve this control through the use of structure and procedure, insisting on rules and policy in order to be accurate and sustain quality.

Individuals of this kind usually have personal codes of behavior. They tend to regard etiquette and tradition as important. Because of their desire for fact and detail, it is also common to find C's have a personal cache of broad general knowledge or very specific knowledge and skills.

High C's can be recognized by the fact they like to do quality work and do it right the first time. They do not like to have to go back and fix something. They are careful, exacting, cautious, systematic, neat, diplomatic, accurate and very tactful.

How It All Works

Rarely, if ever, does someone fit only one characteristic. We all exhibit an influence of each of the styles, but we will have one dominant style. Additionally, depending on the situation, one style may be more of a factor than another. How someone is at work may be different from how they are at home.

Having a deep understanding of the various traits allows you to be a better salesperson if you are aware of your customer's profile. Make no mistake of it; we are all in sales. We may not have the title of Sales Professional, but we are always selling.

On a professional level as a salesperson, I've come to recognize someone who is a High D is going to give you one-word answers. They may not want to talk a lot, but when they are talking, it is about themselves, so my conversation is directed to and about them personally. "How are *you* doing at work?" "How's *your* business?" "How are *you* feeling today?" A customer or patient that is a D will experience a conversation that is directed to the motivations of a D.

With a High I, when I ask a question I have to be prepared for them to talk about anything they want to. They'll cover many topics and points without me saying a word. At times we have to actually control some of our High I patients by asking a question to shift them back to the decision at hand. I's love to talk and interact.

The S's and the C's are the harder ones to read. They are the engineers; they are methodical and diligent, and they are not the one you're going to be selling a lot of Products or Services to the first time around. They're going to ask a lot of questions.

If your style does not match that of an S or C, you may have to speak slower, address specific questions and change the way you interact. For example, I am a High D with a High I. When I am communicating with a High S and C, I have to change the way I talk to accommodate their style. There are occasions I want to get right to the point and if I am dealing with someone who needs to be convinced of something with lots of facts and figures, I need to supply this information if the conversation is going to be productive.

It is during the Warm-Up Stage you find out who the customer is, what behavioral style they possess and what their expectations for interaction will be.

Because of the training we have had in our company, recognizing the strong influencers is very easy; almost second nature. Again, this didn't happen by reading one report or book on the subject. It came from an investment of time and money into specialized training and coaching in order to have a very deep understanding of what drives people. Hands down, this has been one of the major contributing factors to having a highly successful business.

My team and I are also very aware of the differences in serving the first time customer as compared to existing customers. A sad reality is that some entrepreneurs and sales professionals feel new customers are more important than existing customers and put more effort into securing new business rather than continually nurturing their existing clientele.

The fact is an existing customer is extremely valuable to you since they already have a built-in level of trust and confidence. If treated the way they want to be treated they tend to be very loyal and are also an incredible referral system.

Part of the system I previously referred to in our business includes what we do with our existing customers. Before we meet with someone, we review our notes, make certain we are aware of their likes and dislikes, understand their styles based on the DiSC® Classic and we always interact with them based upon their preferences and not ours.

We know what services our customers have had in the past and what their buying habits are. We are aware of our customer's family relationships, their professional talents and their hobbies. All of this review takes place before we meet again so we can get into the Warm-Up Stage in little to no time.

The Warm-Up Stage is *the most essential portion* of the Sales Call; that's where you're cultivating or re-cultivating the relationship with your customer. Don't be tempted to skip the Warm-Up Stage because you are dealing with an existing customer. *All* customers want a relationship before they buy.

With a new customer, you don't have a plethora of information about them. But, if you're lucky to have had a conversation prior to meeting or you have an employee, a coordinator or a scheduling person who has information about that person, you can at least get a feel for how you're going to go into the Warm-Up Stage. This is why our entire team is trained in the DiSC® Classic system. DiSC® Classic is so effective that each of us can identify the DiSC® style of a potential customer over the phone. This is such an asset because we are in the customer's court, connecting and understanding their needs and wants before they walk in the door.

DiSC® Classic profiling comes into play with both existing and new customers. I cannot over-emphasize the value of DiSC® Classic. The ability of my team and partners to identify the different behavioral styles took our practice from good to great. Our emphasis on the DiSC® Classic system took place during the time we decided to intensify our focus on External Marketing.

This was the time we brought in Bob Maccario, the Dental Concierge. We shifted from using the DiSC® Classic as an internal tool for working together as a team to a tool that allowed us to interact effectively with our customer. We learned the importance of knowing our behavior styles in order that we could appropriately adjust the way we interact to meet our customer's needs and comfort level.

DiSC® Classic has helped take us to the point where every year there's growth. Even in the years when most dentists weren't growing, we were experiencing a 10% - 15% annual growth pattern. Our yearly growth is based on several key factors including a deep understanding and use of the customer profiles created using DiSC® Classic. Another is a complete understanding and implementation of *The Success Triangle™*.

To put into perspective how DiSC® Classic impacts what you do, below is an overview of the Four Steps to the Systemized Sales Call as they relate to one's personality.

WARM-UP

Since the Warm-Up Stage is about connecting and building a relationship with your customer, DiSC® Classic can assist you to quickly and deeply connect with your customer. You will know what to ask, what not to ask, how much to interact, when to be formal and when being more at ease is the appropriate approach to take. It even extends into when someone feels comfortable with being touched, say on the shoulder or a pat on the back. Some personality types are extremely comfortable with touch while others would not be at all.

DIALOGUE

The Dialogue is the conversation you have about your Product and Services. The dialogue in essence is your Case/Sales Presentation. After the Warm-Up Stage you move into the Dialogue Stage keeping in mind your customer's predominant DiSC® style. You are deciding how you interact with your customer based on their behavioral style. The Dialogue is talking about your Product or Service, conversing with your customer so they understand what you're offering and, as I say, "Getting them to buy what they want and what they need."

For your existing customers you should resell past purchases of Products or Services to continue to create value or perceived value for their past decisions. It's simply a matter of reviewing the customer's decision and letting them know they made a great choice. It is important to remember that the dialogue changes and is modified based on each person's behavior style.

DISMISSAL

The Dismissal is a shift of gears. We went from relationship building during the Warm-Up, moved to discussing Product benefits and features during the Dialogue. The

Dismissal Stage is so named because I am about to dismiss myself. Before I do, I want to reconnect with the patient and assure them of their decision to buy.

As I'm wrapping up, I reconnect with the patient by doing something like give them my home phone number. I will say to the patient "You can reach me at this number any time." I then re-visit the information I received during the Warm-Up Stage. Not the whole conversation, but parts of it. Maybe the customer is an avid golfer and I now know they are going on a golfing trip. I'd say, "Here's my number, I'll be in touch. Don't hesitate to call me any time at home or at work. And have a great time on your golf trip. I know Myrtle Beach; you're going to love it there. I've played some of those courses." The reason personal conversation is important is that it lets them know you've listened to the what they talked about in the Warm-Up Stage.

I treat the customer as if they are a visitor in my home. I assist them with their coat or purse. I look for ways to help and support them as they are leaving the exam room. Before a patient leaves my presence, I want their last experience of me to be one of appreciation. I want them to know I am grateful for their new or repeat business regardless of their decision to proceed. I am thrilled they took the time to meet with me.

This is where many businesses drop the ball. When you are saying goodbye, be sincere. Avoid any distractions and sincerely connect with them with your final words and actions.

TRANSFER

The Transfer is designed to handle all the financial arrangements. We are transferring the financial obligations and financial responsibilities of the sale to a trained team member.

The customer responsibility for payment is handed to an individual who is efficient in arranging all financial matters concerning the customer. In essence, every step of the way the customer is treated to a methodical process designed to expedite the visit, sale and financial arrangements of their decision and do so in an extremely professional manner.

An area that we have put a lot of attention on is the dialogue from when I transfer a patient from my care to my Patient Coordinator's care. When Bob Maccario trained my team, he focused a great deal on dialogue and language patterns. Over the years, I have incorporated my own style into how I communicate, yet the essence of the dialogue I use during the Transfer was what I learned from Bob.

Once a patient has decided to move forward my dialogue sounds like this, "Becky, since you decided to go with this, here's what I'm going to do. I'm going to give this paperwork to Theresa. Theresa's an expert at getting the finances done. Whatever you and Theresa decide is okay with me as far as how you want to pay for it. Whether you pay over 12 months or three years, Theresa will help you sort that out."

Keep in mind that Theresa has been extensively trained on how to help the customer choose the best payment option. She has full authority to handle these details. Because of her training, experience and commitment to our company, I do not override her decisions. If I did, I would lose her trust and in essence be saying, "You have authority until I decide to take that away from you."

The Transfer is done for many reason and should be done with someone you have introduced to the customer as your coordinator, assistant or financial advisor.

As your team member proceeds with the financial

arrangements, they'll need to form a relationship with your customer based on their behaviors as identified by using DiSC® Classic.

Important factors to keep in mind as to why and how you need to do the Transfer:

- Finance arrangements can take a tremendous amount of time.
- Finances should be handled by a detailed person with high level of empathy.
- The customer may be more open and speak more freely with a third party.
- Many times the salesperson is not the best person to handle the "details" of the purchase.

So, there you have it. The Systemized Sales Call. As I said before, each stage must be done in sequence and completely. However, if you're good at relationship-building (Warm-Up Stage), the other stages are going to go well and require minimal effort. The bottom line is this: if your customers like you, they're going to buy from you.

On the other hand, if you're not good at relationship building, when you transition to the Dialogue Stage, the customer's skepticisms about who you are and how you're selling will surface. If the Dismissal Stage is somewhat rushed and not done professionally, more objections arise. If you're selling a high-ticket item and skip the Transfer Stage and/or don't offer a way to make financing available the whole sales process is flawed.

Like *The Success Triangle™*, each stage of the Systemized Sales Call is designed to support and potentiate the other. If one stage is weak, the others are less effective.

Implementing a Systemized Sales Call and Systemized

Sales Presentation usually feels unnatural at first. It requires practice and patience to sound spontaneous and not rehearsed. With enough practice, it becomes effortless and is just like having a conversation with someone. It's like I'm talking to you about the Phillies baseball game. "Hey, did you hear that...?" "Boy, you know what...?" "Look at that..." "Take a look at this..." "Look at the way that tooth is..." "You need three crowns here. You know, I think the best thing to do is correct this one first and then this one." The conversation has to become natural and authentic throughout.

What has helped considerably is that we put time aside to practice the process. We will role-play patient scenarios among team members so we have a sense of what is to happen, in which order and at what speed.

I want every customer to have a pleasant and professional experience from the moment they enter our office until the moment they leave. By now, you know we take pride in our building, our team and our service. We treat our customers like family with the utmost respect and appreciation. Our team is always engaged in professional development of some type including training to use the DiSC® Classic as well as the Systemized Sales Call and the Systemized Sales Presentation.

I must also point out we pride ourselves in having a professional team that understands the value of a personal connection. As well educated as everyone is in the DiSC® Classic system, the Systemized Sales Call and *The Success Triangle™*, we all recognize that true care and empathy cannot be learned. Care and compassion are given freely. It doesn't matter what you are selling; all systems and structures, if not accompanied by a team that sincerely respects their customers, will eventually backfire on you.

A huge part of the process of sales success is to couple a great Sales Call with a polished Sales Presentation or what I have coined the Systemized Sales Presentation. To be successful in the Systemized Sales Presentation there are four key elements you must address with your customer in order to achieve optimum results: Attention, Interest, Desire, and Action. We'll explore this in the next chapter.

SYSTEMIZED SALES CALL
SUCCESS SUMMARY

1. Know as much about your customer prior to making your contact or call.
2. Follow a sequence to systemize your Sales Call:
   a. Warm-Up
   b. Dialogue
   c. Dismissal
   d. Transfer
   Following the sequence and scripts creates the system that makes the delivery go from unnatural to natural behavior.
3. The Warm-Up is the most important piece of the Sales Call.
4. The Warm-Up is when you form your relationship with the customer based on their DiSC® behavior style.
5. The Dialogue links to the Systemized Sales Call.
6. The Dialogue is also a time to re-sell past purchases, Products or Services.
7. The Dialogue is the time to establish Value or

Perceived Value for your Product or Service.

8. The Dismissal is the time to once again discuss some of the Warm-Up topics and strengthen your relationship. It lets your customer know you listened.

9. The Dismissal is brief but important.

10. The Transfer gives the financial responsibilities to someone trained in financial arrangements.

11. The Transfer is important if you are uncomfortable dealing with money or you do not have the time.

12. A specific scripted dialogue is needed for the Transfer.

13. When a Systemized Sales Call is done effectively, you create Trust and Confidence with your customer.

14. Creating Trust and Confidence with your customer leads to a higher closure rate when doing your Systemized Sales Presentation.

CHAPTER 7

Systemized Sales Presentation

As much as the Systemized Sales Call is essential to the success of your business, so is the Systemized Sales Presentation.

As with the Sales Call, I found a systemized approach to the Sales Presentation will produce greater customer acceptance and a higher closing ratio. The intention of the Systemized Sales Presentation is to give the customer what they need and what they want.

I cannot emphasize enough how important honesty and ethics are when selling. A Systemized Sales Presentation could almost be construed as an attempt to control your customer. Some might say, "You're doing something to make him or her say 'yes' and you're doing this in a manipulative way."

Honesty has to be at the foundation of any Sales

Presentation. If you're selling life insurance and a person needs only a million dollars worth of coverage and you try to sell them two million, shame on you. That's fraud, that's illegal, that's wrong, and you shouldn't do it. Simple as that.

If I'm telling someone they should have veneers or change certain things in their mouth because I want to line my pocket, that's wrong and it will come back to bite me. That's not what I'm talking about when I speak of a Systemized Sales Presentation. I'm talking about a system whereby we're helping people get to yes; yes to something the customer wants or needs and it is going to make their life better. In the process, I just happen to make money.

Money comes and goes, but the benefit the person receives is long lasting and personally empowering. If you want to have long-term success, the value and service you provide has to serve the customer more than it serves you.

That is why I refer to sales as "strategic influence." You are influencing someone and they're influencing you at the same time. We have a responsibility as sales professionals to use our influence in the best way possible. The difference between manipulation and influence is intention; the intention has to be one of service and integrity. Influence with integrity and always have the other person's highest good in mind.

The design of our Sales Presentation is to comfortably further a process of benefit, not push someone into something they do not want. The customer must always be benefitted with more value and service than you receive in financial compensation. The customer must always be number one.

The Systemized Sales Presentation has been designed to meet the needs of our patients but can be adopted by any industry or sales profession. As with the Systemized Sales Call, you'll note there are four steps to the Sales Presentation. All four steps must be done with competence, confidence and in order. The Four Steps of a Systemized Sales Presentation:

1. Gaining Customer *Attention*
2. Generating Customer *Interest*
3. Cultivating Customer *Desire*
4. Moving the Customer to *Action*

Charlie Schaivo taught me this process. It is now the cornerstone of *The Success Triangle*™ and the Systemized Sales Presentation. It is the core of what I teach in my sales training and business building courses.

Like everything worthwhile in life, the Systemized Sales Presentation did not happen overnight. Although I learned this process nearly 25 years ago, it was over the process of time it became an integral part of my overall business system.

In 1983, Charlie would come to the office and we would role-play with one of us in the chair. If we were presenting a crown or bridge, we had slides that showed the before and after treatments. We would use certain slides to grab a patient's attention. We'd use both slides and dialogue to generate interest and we would practice how to answer questions and handle objections in order to cultivate desire and then move our customer to action. We practiced and role-played until it was second nature.

After years of practice, everything I say is memorized, done in a sequence, and designed to support the next step in the Systemized Sales Presentation. Every step is thought-out, creating a synergistic effect and a high closure rate. I'm committed to continually perfecting my Sales Presentation.

Most people would not think a dentist has to "sell" their services. However, just like you, I'm in the game of selling. Dentists have to build their businesses and clientele (patients) just like everyone else.

As in most industries, we must embrace selling as a professional skill. Not everyone in my industry has been quick to see the light. Many dentists simply maintain the status quo and are living a slow, painful death. It is no longer just important but critical in my industry that we help people say YES to the Products or Services they want and need.

As a dentist, I use this Systemized Sales Presentation to present basic dentistry, cosmetic dentistry and restorative dentistry to my patients. Depending on what area of dentistry the patient needs, I use different verbiage, but the four steps remain the same: Attention, Interest, Desire, and Action.

GRAB THEIR ATTENTION AND GENERATE INTEREST

Whenever we are selling, we must first get someone's attention and generate interest for our Product.

As an example, when introducing a full or partial cosmetic smile makeover, if I have a patient in the chair I may say, "Are you happy with the appearance of your teeth?"

If they say, "Yes, I am happy with the appearance of my teeth," and they have crooked teeth, I may say, "Well, you know, there are things that can be done to improve the unevenness of some of the teeth. Would you like to see some photographs of people who had problems like yours that we fixed?" If they say: "No, I like the way my teeth look," that is the end of the conversation. I'm done and they're happy.

On the other hand if they say, "Well, what do you mean?" or "Yes, I'd like to see that," then I have a book of *Before* and *After* pictures of patients who had specific problems; whether it be spaces, crooked teeth, dark teeth, old fillings, old crowns, etc. I've grabbed their attention by showing them the photos.

Because I have systemized the sales presentation, I have memorized the location of each photo in the book. I know exactly where specific case photos are located so that I can quickly and efficiently show them the *Before* and *After* scenarios.

If the photo I want to show the customer is in the back of the book, I start at the front. I do this because I now have the opportunity to show my patient many photos of people who are satisfied customers. Attention first and now Interest starts to pique! It is not uncommon for the patient in the chair to say, "Oh, wow, let me see that," or "How did you do that?"

If I know the photo I'm looking for is in the front of the book, I start at the back. This way the patient is now getting to see pictures of what I've done. If I show the picture at the front first, they will miss the opportunity to see the rest. This isn't unlike many industries that display pictures of their work and of satisfied customers in some sort of visual layout.

In fact, I have a friend who told me when she was picking out her kitchen, the sales clerk said, "You know, I have pictures of kitchens like yours we've done. Let me show you our book." He had her look through the whole book using a process similar to mine before she made a decision.

One of my greatest attention getters is asking the right questions and having photos to reference. After I have their attention, a great way to grab their interest is by offering an image of the patient to show them how they could look if they choose to get the treatment. It's all done through the magic of computer imaging.

I ask my patients if this would be something they're interested in. If they say yes, then I take their picture and do an imaging. With this technology, they get to see what they're going to look like before the treatment is ever done. This piques their interest.

Because the process can take some time, I give them two options of how they want to receive the pictures. I can either send them their picture or have them in for a consultation in the not too distant future. The reason I offer the choice of how they want to receive the images is my sales process is not at all high pressure. Again, it is about helping the customer make the right decision for them.

This type of process could be compared to an image an architect would create of someone's dream home or a landscaper of a client's yard. You are giving the client the opportunity to visualize and see what they will get.

At that point, the customer is sufficiently engaged and will move the process along. During the follow up visit, the customer will present you with some questions and how you answer them leads you to the next crucial step: creating Desire.

Our patients will usually ask, "Well, what's the next step?" That's a strong indicator of Desire and they're ready to go ahead. Other questions that point to Desire are:

"What do I have to do to get these results?"

"What are you going to do to my teeth?"

"How long does it take?"

"How long does it last?"

"How much does it cost?"

"How many teeth do I need to do?"

"Does it hurt?"

"How do I pay for it?"

There are usually seven to eight questions our patients or customers will ask indicating desire. This is true in most any business whether you are selling kitchens, computers or insurance. Ninety-nine percent of the time there are questions your customers will ask that are specific to your industry. You need to know the questions and how to answer them in a sincere, natural, and confidence building way. If you answer those questions incorrectly, too quickly or in an inappropriate fashion, you may not create desire and you can lose the sale.

Being prepared with answers to the most frequently asked questions is what a true sales professional will study, learn and role-play so that the process with the customer becomes very natural. If you grab their Attention, generate Interest, and answer their questions in a skilled way, you are going to create Desire. Desire always leads to Action!

Action is easy! In our company, Action goes hand in hand with the part of the sales call that is referred to as the Transfer. This is where we will be asking our customer to sign on the dotted line.

As I mentioned, it may be necessary to make various financial payment options available to your customers. As a dentist, I have specific ways patients can make financial arrangements. We introduce them to the financial coordinator (this is the Transfer) and that's where the action happens. Our coordinator walks them through all the action steps to finalize the sale by helping the customer to secure an appropriate financial arrangement.

This person must be highly skilled and well trained to handle the payment and financial arrangements. As with any part of the process, you cannot leave the Action step to chance. You must put money, time and effort into training your team every step of the way.

This is how we get Attention, Interest, Desire, and Action for cosmetic dentistry. It's similar for restorative dentistry, just a different Attention-grabber and a different Interest-getter. But the final two steps, gaining Desire and taking Action, are the same because the customer is going to ask the same questions about money and they will have to take Action about financing. In any business, you have to find your own Attention-grabber and create your own Interest-getter.

Desire and Action are the same for almost every sales process regardless of the business. Every interested customer will ask certain questions. A good salesperson will know the questions their customers will ask and be fluent with his or her answers. They'll also be able to answer the specific question according to the customer's DiSC® behavioral style. This is critical.

If a D person who is direct and to the point says to me, "How much does it cost and how long is it going to take?" I say, "It costs this much and it's going to take this amount of time." That's the answer. Quick question, quick answer.

If a High C person who wants a lot of detail asks me the question, "How much does it cost and how long is it going to take?" I don't say, "It costs this much." I would take some time and say, "Well, you know, to do this type of work there is a lot of time involved and it's a very detailed procedure. I use a high-quality laboratory where the best work is done." I'd go into detail about the procedure itself. I'm giving them the same answer I'd give a D, but it takes a different period of time and requires greater detail. The question is important, but the way you answer the question based on a DiSC® Classic profile is more important.

A High D person may just say, "When could we get started?" They may not ask you how much it is because they may not even care about cost, they just want to get it done; they want the end result.

The High I person may say, "I have to meet a lot of people and I'm concerned how I'll look in the interim." I'll say, "Don't worry; you'll have temporaries and you'll look just fine. You're going to look great in front of people."

The S and C profile types are going to be worried about the quality of the work and how long it's going to last. It isn't any different in your business. Your customers will have specific concerns based upon their DiSC® Classic profile and it is your job to address those concerns based on their style, not yours.

Know your questions, know your answers, and know how to deliver the answer in four different ways based on their DiSC® behavior style. Even though you are presenting the same information, one question can be answered in four different ways.

It's also important not only to follow the Attention, Interest, Desire and Action steps, it's equally important to do them in the right sequence. You must not skip any steps or the order of the steps. This takes practice!

We've talked about what we do and what we say, but we have not discussed the actual performance. In the dental world, just like in your world, customers have comfort zones. Part of the Systemized Sales Presentation is to understand and utilize the physical dynamics of the customer relationship. When I talk to a patient, I'm not washing my hands looking over my shoulder. I wash my hands first, then I sit down; not above the person so I'm looking down at them, I sit down eye-to-eye and knee-to-knee. This is a comfortable distance for most folks.

With I and D profiles, I can sit even closer and I can touch them, say on the shoulder or knee. The S and C profiles require a greater distance between people; you have to be further away from these folks. I'm going to sit down and speak to them at a distance and at a speed where they can pace the conversation with ease.

The Sales Presentation takes a keen awareness of relationships and the dynamics that accompany them.

I just had an experience that drove home how important relationship dynamics are. I had a sales call by a radio station. Unfortunately, I was less than impressed. They sent two salespeople out; one's the rookie and one's the expert. The rookie is obviously in training. So the expert's sitting there; he's looking real sharp in his thousand-dollar suit and the other guy's dressed a bit lower end and comes across as the nice guy.

The seasoned guy is talking to me, but he's looking out the window more than he's looking at me. Mid-way through the sales call I turned him off.

He didn't look at me and tried to rush me before I was ready to make a decision. He asked me tie-down questions inappropriately and asked for the sale before he got my full attention and interest. I found his questions insulting because they were premature and very canned.

"What could we do to have you sign today?" He was closing me before I had enough information, he was out of sequence with his sales presentation — everything was wrong, inappropriate and insulting. Because he doesn't seem to be sincerely interested in me, I wouldn't buy dirt from him if I needed to plant a flower.

Now, I did say you have to rehearse answers, but you also have to know the personality type you are addressing and most importantly, treat the person or persons you are talking to with the utmost respect. To simply have canned answers makes your sales presentation less than professional and plays into the stereotype many people have formulated about slick salespeople.

Let's put it into context with your customers. If you meet your customer in their office, you are now in their territory; you're their guest. You shake their hand and ask, "Is it okay to sit here?" Only upon being given permission do you sit down. You are etiquette-wise and courteous above and beyond the norm. When you talk to your potential customer, you'll talk to them in a way they can relate to matching their DiSC® behavioral style.

Consider the same principle using the example of a restaurant owner. Let's say I own a restaurant and the two radio salespeople want to sell me some airtime. First, they have to get a sense of my personality. Then, to get my attention, they would show sample commercials and dialogue and some of the results that they've had with other restaurants.

A popular restaurant in many areas of the United States is *Ruth's Chris Steak House*. If Ruth's Chris has advertised with them and my restaurant is along the lines of a Ruth's Chris establishment, they could bring in a portfolio that shows examples of commercial scripts from satisfied clients and how they ran other successful advertising campaigns with this high-end restaurant.

Once they get a sense of my personality, they proceed to get my attention as they flip through the book and say, "These are businesses who have advertised on our radio station and have been very happy with what we've done for them. They have been so happy with the results they are repeat customers."

Once I have given them permission to proceed, they could go on to give specific examples of how they helped the restaurant have great results with their advertising. "They advertise during the sports show because a lot of men like steakhouses and we've put them on the air during that time." That would be the attention-getter. Getting a prospect's undivided attention is a necessity if you're going to succeed in the sale.

The first few minutes are the most important part of the whole presentation. First impressions carry a lot of weight. For this reason, you should focus your remarks on what interests the prospect and therefore link their attention infallibly to you. You'll find most salespeople violate this rule.

I've found many salespeople get in a rut and approach their potential customers in a more or less haphazard way. They do not have a well thought-out and specific attention-getting opener. To avoid shooting from the hip we have customized and systemized our attention-getters and you should do the same.

Keep in mind to be effective you must get the customer's attention quickly and completely. Never forget today's customer is very savvy; no longer are they easily swayed by the inauthentic or slick sales call. Customers want to interact with authentic sales professionals and be assured they are receiving a quality product. To link a potential customer's attention to you, you must make a statement that truly interests him or her.

Virtually anyone who has been in sales for any length of time has been trained in the "Ask 'em about the weather" scenario or, seeing a picture on their desk, saying, "Is that your family?" Do you think a prospect is really interested in the weather if you are asking the question just to make small talk?

Chances are he or she is not unless something about the weather is directly impacting the prospect. With the picture dialogue, the family question may be obvious to the point of being insulting.

Again, you must link the prospect or customer's attention to what you will be presenting. You can do this in several ways by:

- Paying a sincere compliment
- Asking a relevant question
- Introducing the element of suspense
- Making an appropriate reference to a well-known person or situation
- Displaying action
- Giving helpful ideas

I recommend you practice all types of attention-getting statements before you decide on a few best suited to your potential customer and to your industry.

To gain and sustain a prospect's interest, your sales presentation should be directed to more than one sense: not just hearing but also sight, smell, taste, and touch. You should not only speak, but also demonstrate. When I show my customers Before and After pictures, I show them pictures of somebody else to get their attention. Customer privacy is very important, so always get permission when using their picture as an example or to close a sale. In some industries, it's the law.

To get their interest, I show them pictures of themselves. Back to the restaurant example and the radio reps, I would use examples of their business, not someone else's. If I'm the sales professional for the radio station and I'm dealing with a restaurant, I'm going to shift from discussing other restaurants and say, "Okay, now let's talk about your restaurant. In your restaurant, what do you hope to achieve? Do you hope to corner the baby boomers or are you going for senior citizens? What type of clientele do you want to attract?"

The prospect might say, "I'm looking to do the high-end thing. I'm looking to get the baby boomers."

I respond with, "Let me show you this. This is what we will say about your restaurant. These words have worked, this dialogue has worked and this is what we will script for you on the radio."

That got their interest. The next step would be to gain desire. "Mr. Restaurant Owner, do you have any questions about what we've talked about today?"

"Yeah, how many days would this commercial air? How much is it going to cost? What financial payment options are there? Who pays for the production of the ad?" These are the same questions other prospects and customers have likely asked on every other sales call.

When these questions are answered in a skilled way according to the customer's DiSC® Classic profile, Desire has been created.

The Action is discussing the cost of the Product or Service and how the customer is going to pay for it. At that time, we do a Transfer. Our coordinator discusses the way the financing is handle. Ultimately, she asks for the financial commitment. That's how you get the Action.

In some cases, you may not have an actual coordinator so you have to be flexible enough to handle a smooth transition on how you move to this step. It can't be rigid or forced. Unfortunately, this is where many salespeople get very uncomfortable and it shows. As with every other aspect of what you do, practice this step until it becomes second nature and you actually enjoy doing this.

If you are uncomfortable with the financial end of selling, there may be a couple of primary reasons. For instance, you may not really believe what you are selling is worth the price. This leads into the second reason; you don't understand the true value your Product or Service offers to your customer. To be a top-notch sales professional, you must believe wholeheartedly in your offerings. If you don't, you will never succeed at a high level.

To recap, here is the simple yet effective order of the Systemized Sales Presentation.

- **Attention** – To get a customer's attention, offer similar examples of previous customers and what you've done for them. The more examples you have to choose from the better off you will be.
- **Interest** – To pique a customer's interest, show them what you can do for them.
- **Desire** – To generate desire, answer your customer's questions in a very particular way specific to their DiSC® Classic profile.
- **Action** – Action requires a request to move forward and secure a financial commitment.

Recently I was on the receiving end of an outstanding sales presentation and found it quite incredible. I went window-shopping for a higher-end SUV. I walked into the Infiniti dealer with no intention to buy, yet I wasn't closed to the idea of buying. When I walked onto the showroom floor, the dialogue went something like this.

The salesman said, "How are you today? What can I do for you? What are you interested in seeing?"

"I'm interested in seeing SUVs."

"Oh, do you know anything about the SUVs we have here?"

"No."

"Well, I'd like to show you the different types of SUVs we have. Would that be okay?" He got my permission to sell me. Permission selling is very popular and important. *This was a great way to grab my attention as we moved forward.*

The salesman started to get my attention when he showed me the SUVs and then said, "This Infiniti is a beautiful and distinctive car." The word Infiniti really got my attention because I enjoy top of the line vehicles.

We discussed the product line; what is included on the Infiniti; why the Infiniti is a better SUV than the other high end SUVs; what sets the Infiniti apart from the other makes and models. We also talked about what set this particular dealership apart from other dealerships. This sales presentation was done in a friendly way and with very low pressure.

The salesman got my attention by telling me about the quality of the Infiniti, some of the features that the Infiniti has over the other cars, and the benefits of dealing with this particular dealership.

He really got my interest when I drove the car. As I'm driving, I'm remembering what he told me about the car, what he told me about the dealership, what he told me about himself, and I'm liking it all. Once I'm through driving I begin to ask specific questions:

"What kind of mileage does it get?"

"What is included in the warranty?"

"Does it have side panel airbags?"

"How safe is it for my family?"

"What are the industry ratings?"

He answers my questions in a very comfortable, non-threatening way. He's not talking down to me and he's not talking up either. Everything was easy. His behavior was very much like my behavior pattern, so it was easy to ask questions and it was easy to get answers. Then we got down to, "What's the best price on this car?" My desire was showing.

After going back and forth for several minutes, I finally said, "If you can sell it for this price, I'll buy it today," and we sealed the deal. Within less than three hours on a rainy day, I bought a $44,000 car even though I still had another car I wasn't ready to get rid of. But I liked everything that happened that day.

I didn't go there to buy a car. I went there to look at a car. Yet, I was obviously in the market if I bought the vehicle. What I can tell you is had the salesperson not approached me the way he did and made the experience comfortable for me, the customer, I would never have even considered buying the car that day.

This is a perfect example of everything going as planned. All four steps were brilliantly executed from grabbing my attention, interest and desire to taking the necessary action. This is how all sales presentations should be: systemized, comfortable and successful.

BARRIERS OF PERCEPTION

Not all salespeople are as competent as the gentleman I bought my Infiniti from. Many salespeople lose a sale based upon their own barriers of perception. There is a tendency to form first impressions about our customers that may not be accurate. I've witnessed many a lost sale because of a false assumption. Admittedly, I have also been guilty of this myself.

When I see a patient who comes in who isn't dressed

well, may be really young or a senior citizen, I may be tempted to prejudge their ability to buy or desire to buy based on my preconceived notions. I learned early on you never know for sure what someone is capable of and willing to do based on appearances. Every salesperson can fall into the trap of stereotyping their customers.

If you pre-judge any customer based on gender, age, attire, or looks, you are losing sales. The way someone looks doesn't always equate to his or her ability to buy or their purchasing power.

I also learned along the way not to tell people, "You need this! You should get this!" Today I've learned to say, "I think these are the one or two best options that would help you." I offer choices to my customers, I do not dictate. However, if I see them going in what I truly believe is the wrong direction, or if they've come to a conclusion that is not in their best interest, I will tell them, "You know, I will honor your wishes because you're the customer and you can do whatever you think is best for you. I will do this procedure, as long as you understand this may not be the best approach. We may have to do something down the road that's going to be different than what you've chosen today."

You must have the ability to tell the truth about their decision without making the customer feel bad. The dialogue I use is, "You know, Mrs. Jones, you've chosen to patch this problem for now. I understand based on your present financial situation this is the best choice for you. I think you've made a good choice because what we're going to do is put you in a holding pattern. By that I mean we're going to do the minimum; just enough so you don't get in trouble."

Never embarrass the customer or make them feel bad. "At some point in the future perhaps you will choose this other option when your finances allow. So let's do this. Let's just patch you up so you're going to be functional and you can use these teeth for a little bit longer. Maybe things will get better down the road and you could go ahead with the ideal treatment."

When a patient doesn't go ahead with what I suggest, I don't embarrass or pressure them. We've all heard, "Well, if you don't want it, that's just up to you. I'll just sell it to somebody else." I'm floored that we still encounter salespeople who have the audacity to respond in such a fashion.

I understand not all customers can afford the best. Once you go through all the steps it could be that someone just doesn't have the money. I've sold them, but there's no action because when we get to discussing payment and taking action they say, "Doc, I never thought it would be ten thousand. I thought we were going to be talking about a thousand bucks to do my teeth."

As disappointing as that can be, I'm always quick to say, "You know what? Maybe things will be better in the future for you. Things change." If the procedures they are wanting are more for looks than health, I absolutely won't push. If it's a health issue, that's completely different. In that case, I'm obligated to encourage the treatment even if their finances are tight.

If it's appropriate, I'll sometimes make suggestions on how to get the money. If it's an older person, I'll say to them, "You know, I've had other patients who go to their children when they need services like this. You've helped your children through life and maybe it's time for them to help you," or, "Do you have a relative that could help you get this work done?"

If the answer is, "No, Doc, I have nobody left," then I go back to my standard dialogue. I say, "Okay, let's do this. Let's put you in a holding pattern. By that, I mean we're going to patch you up and do the minimum; just enough so you don't lose your teeth and you don't get in trouble. Maybe down the road things will be better for you and you'll be able to get this work done."

I don't push people, I lead them. I lead them to where they should be. Sometimes we don't get there because they don't want to follow me. If a customer doesn't follow that is okay because not everybody buys and not everybody wants the best. It's as simple as that.

Sometimes it's not an issue of whether or not they can afford a procedure. There are some people who have such a low self-esteem they don't feel they deserve the best. There are also people that don't value dentistry, they don't value cars, they don't value computers and they want the cheapest of everything because that's the way they've lived their whole life.

Your sales presentation isn't going to change core beliefs. If someone thinks they need a cheap, old car and you try to sell them a Mercedes because you believe it's the best car, they're never buying a Mercedes.

If I tell a customer they should get veneers and they've never spent a dime on their teeth, they won't get veneers. Their goal is to spend the minimum amount of money on their teeth, whether they fall out or not. The customer will make decisions based on their core beliefs.

Core beliefs can be influenced by what the person has grown up with; what their experience has been. Let's say their mother never took care of her teeth and her teeth fell out. They may have learned that this was acceptable dental care so it will likely be a core belief. I can't change what's inside that person. I can only lead them so far. What I do know is if I follow these four steps, I can take people who are on the fence and get them off. I can get them to do something good for themselves. I can also educate someone who doesn't know what is best and that's really where the key is; that's where our responsibility rests. It is to educate and to offer the best. The choice is theirs.

DECISION MAKERS

I'm also very pro-active in identifying the decision maker. You can waste a lot of time if you don't know who the decision maker is. To find out, I just ask.

As I get to a certain place in my Sales Presentation with a customer who is married, I say, "Is your husband or wife with you today?"

"No."

"Is this something you want to discuss with them, or are you going to make the decision?"

"Oh no, my husband/wife and I do everything together."

"Well, let's do this. Let's have you back with your husband/wife and we'll go through this together."

I don't limit these types of questions solely to female or male customers. You have some couples where decisions are made independent of one another and depending on the dynamics of a relationship, large financial investments may require both people be a part of the decision making process.

You do, however, have to ask in an appropriate way. You don't want to say, "Who makes the decisions in the house, you or your husband?"

I always ask, "Is your husband or wife with you?"

"No."

"Is it important they be here with you to go ahead?"

"No, I'll make this decision."

"Great, let me show you what your options are."

I simply ask who makes the decisions, but I do it in a way that is comfortable and easy for the customer.

PRACTICE

As with anything, the more you do something the better you get. This process can initially feel a bit unnatural. In our office, we role-play every possible patient scenario. When I am the patient in the chair, I can be pretty obstinate and make it as tough as possible for my team member: "What do you mean it costs a thousand dollars? I'm not paying a thousand dollars for teeth!" One of the most effective ways to do role-playing is to work with other team members that know all of the obstacles and objections your customers have.

An important part of my sales training seminars is to have participants practice and role-play. We do this so that a new behavior that may initially feel awkward and unnatural becomes second nature and feels natural. Ultimately, becoming highly competent at sales is about getting to a place where what was once an unnatural (or conscious) behavior becomes natural and unconscious.

Up until now, our focus has been mainly on what is required to have success in business. Let's shift gears from talking just about business success and move into a discussion that covers both business and personal success to give you *TOTAL SUCCESS*.

SYSTEMIZED SALES PRESENTATION
SUCCESS SUMMARY

1. We are all in sales, selling a Product, Service or idea.
2. The success of your business and life is directly proportional to your ability to sell and market.
3. Sales is NOT manipulation. It is strategic influence. Make statements that help your customer get what they want or need.
4. Follow a sequence to systemize your sales presentation:
   a. Attention
   b. Interest
   c. Desire
   d. Action

   Each step links to the next and it is important to follow the sequence to increase your closure rate. It is more difficult to get Desire and Action if you do not gain Attention or generate Interest.

   Following a sequence and scripts helps you develop a Systemized Sales Call and your unnatural behavior becomes natural behavior. You develop unnatural natural behavior.
5. Talk to the decision maker.
6. Present your Product or Service based on the customer's DiSC® Classic profile.
7. The Systemized Sales Presentation links to the Dialogue in the Systemized Sales Call.
8. Getting your customer's Attention requires skill. You may need to show how your Product or Service

helped other customers.

9. To generate Interest, show the customer what you can do for them.

10. To cultivate Desire, know the questions your customer will ask and answer the question according to the customer's DiSC® Classic profile. One question could be answered three or four different ways.

11. Moving the customer requires you to ask the customer to move forward in the process and explain the costs and financing.

12. Show empathy if the customer truly cannot move ahead.

13. When value has been established and the customer will truly benefit, we have an obligation to help them to say, "Yes."

CHAPTER 8

Five Part Formula for Success

Success is not single sided; it is a holistic experience taking into account all of life's experiences. I view success as a Five Part Formula. Our conversation about success starts with business, but ends with the total life experience.

If I asked a group of people to write down everything they needed for success in business and life we could probably fill countless whiteboards, blackboards, flipcharts, computer files and notepads. I have found there are only five basic skills needed in order to be successful:

1. Become an Expert / Have a Great Product and/or Service
2. Develop Sales and Marketing Skills
3. Get Help from Experts (Mentors)
4. Control Your Thoughts
5. Create Balance in Your Life

Each part is equally important to the others as they support a balance of business success and life success. Business and life successes are not exclusive of one another. When you have both, there is a synergy so that you have greater *TOTAL SUCCESS* as opposed to success in individual parts.

Of the five basic skills listed for success, money is not included for specific reasons. Success is not a result of making money; making money is a result of success. Money is not necessarily a part of success; it can be a way of keeping score. I truly believe that success is the result of providing value and service. We are paid based on the amount of value and service we provide. Money is a measure of that value and service.

When we work with our customers, we should be paid directly for the amount of value and service we provide. In reality, we should be providing *more* value and service than we are being paid. If you do that, money will never be an issue. You will always be paid the fee you deserve because you are providing more to your customer based on the amount of value and service you provide to them. Henry Ford said, "Wealth, like happiness, is never attained when sought after directly. It comes as a byproduct of providing a useful service."

The reason I know that money is not part of success is because one of the most successful people I know is my father. My father worked in a factory and never had the opportunity to make much money. Yet he is still a success.

If you are in a position of a professional or you have the type of job where you can make a good living, you *should* be making money. In fact, you have an obligation to yourself and your family to make money. If you are performing in your job to the fullest extent or with the greatest skills it could be done, you will make money. If you are not, you are cheating yourself and your family. It's like the Biblical story where the servants were given money from their master. The gold they were given symbolized talents. Two servants worked with the money, made more and were praised. They used their talents. The one who didn't invest the money but instead buried the gold and did nothing with it was admonished and his gold was taken away and given to the servants who made use of the gold. If we have been given talents and do not use them, we are cheating ourselves and, in the end, the customer.

If you never graduated from high school and you work in a factory, you may not have the opportunity to make a lot of money, but that does not mean you cannot be successful. You can still have the components in your life to be a successful person. However, if the people who have been given the talents to make money don't do it, they are cheating themselves by not applying themselves to their fullest extent and making money. Again, success is not the result of making money, making money is the result of success. Success is the result of providing value and service. Money measures the amount of value and service that you provide. Simply put, when you provide value and service, you will be successful and make money.

Although there have been many words and pages already dedicated to the first three parts of the formula, they are so important they bear repeating. Looking at the five parts you would find the following:

BECOME AN EXPERT
HAVE A GREAT PRODUCT AND/OR SERVICE

Expertise is not easy to come by and many people fool

themselves into thinking their knowledge is adequate and self-designate their level of skill as that of an "expert." Some people believe because they fulfilled a required curriculum or passed a test they are suddenly an expert. It is not uncommon upon completion of dental school that some dentists think they know everything they need to know. In reality, they know very little.

Markets change and demands for the service you provide changes. If you don't recognize the market shift or change in demand for what you are doing you will be left behind. This is true for any industry.

At some point I knew that if I wanted to be an expert dentist, and more specifically a cosmetic dentist, I had to get specialized training. There were four places I could have gone for the next level of training. I chose The Las Vegas Institute of Advanced Dental Studies (LVI) because I liked their philosophy and what they had to offer.

In the last few years alone, I took multiple courses that cost hundreds of thousands of dollars in time and expense to become a cosmetic dentist. It was a major commitment and one I was willing to make. Anyone who is an expert in their field has to make an incredible commitment of time, money and energy. It doesn't just happen by chance. I also discovered along the way that as I focused on improving my skills as a cosmetic dentist my skills as a general dentist improved.

Developing a high level of expertise was really a matter of vision for me. In the last eight years I knew I wanted to do more cosmetic dentistry. I was intrigued by what was possible and instinctively knew I had to learn more. The standard curriculum no longer met my needs and I needed more professional training.

I also realized early on that improving my overall ability is about being fair to my patient. Everybody, no matter what industry they are in, needs to be on top of their game. If you're not at the top of your game, you're not being fair to your customer. It may not mean you are giving them an inferior product, but you're certainly not giving them the highest quality of service.

I've discovered many folks balk at continued education and advanced training. They are captured by a mind-set that whispers, "I don't deserve to spend that kind of money on myself," or "I'll just get by." I've found these folks are usually worried about what they're giving up, mainly in dollars, as opposed to what they're going to get.

> **COMPETENCE INCREASES CONFIDENCE**
>
> **CONFIDENCE INCREASES COMPETENCE**

By investing in your own training and education, you will gain more in the long run than you're giving up. With increased skill comes increased confidence. With increased confidence comes increased competence. The rewards will continue to multiply.

Many are comfortable with the status quo. They feel because they've been at something for a long time it qualifies them as an expert. I learned a long time ago just because you've got a lot of years in or you've done something repeatedly, that doesn't necessarily make you an expert. Some people work in a vacuum doing the same thing day in and day out thinking they are the best at what they do. Wrong!

You can't increase your expertise on your own; someone

has to teach you. I don't care if you're already at the top of your game, there's somebody that's on top of you that's doing it better. That's the person you have to talk to!

This is about your Service, your Product and the level at which you deliver. Years ago I heard a saying that has stayed with me, "If you're not moving ahead, you're moving backwards or you're dying." I know as long as I'm fixing teeth, I'm going to be focused on learning a new and better way and definitely keep up with the latest and greatest techniques and technology.

If someone wants to be considered an expert, they have to put constant effort into learning all they can about what they do, what their customers need and what the market demands.

DEVELOP SALES AND MARKETING SKILLS

The success of your business is directly proportionate to your ability to sell and market. Taking that one step further, I believe the success of your life is directly proportionate to your ability to sell and market. The better you sell and market the higher level of success you will attain.

I'm not talking about selling used cars. I'm talking about selling your Services, Products or ideas. Additionally, you are selling your philosophies, your principles to your children and selling to make relationships with your spouse and family better. I'm talking about selling Products and Services they want and need that are going to make them better people. Sales and marketing is not about you getting something; it is about you *giving* something.

Sales is a kind of strategic influence. Too many times we think of sales as manipulation because we have the vision of the slick salesperson; the person who's trying to sell for his or her good and not for the good of the customer. Sales is about benefits and coming to a mutual agreement with your customer that what you have to offer is of value. Once value has been established, you have the responsibility to influence the person to say, "Yes."

You always have to have the other person's highest good in mind. In fact, Charlie used to tell me about the U Attitude. When he first presented the U Attitude idea, it was foreign to me.

He would sit in front of me, hold his pad of paper and he'd draw a U. One part of the U started with the customer coming to me and it ended back with the customer to complete the U.

This means the process has to start with the customer, come to me, and then go back to the customer. The customer always has to be the person who benefits the most in the sales process and the U Attitude has helped me to remember this over the years.

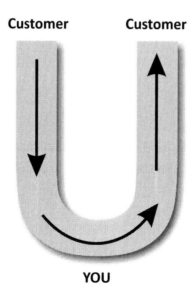

Customer   **Customer**

YOU

Selling is about helping the client. The times I have been sold by people who have good sales skills is fantastic; a great experience. They see what I want and what I need. They know how I'm going to benefit by it and they help me get there.

Sales requires compassion, understanding, and talking in such a way people are comfortable dealing with you. When you create comfort for your customer, they will return again and again. Most of my patients do business with me because they say they trust me. They'll say, "If that's what I need, I trust you know what is best." They have put their faith in me and I'm not about to let them down.

Selling isn't rocket science, but it is a powerful skill. I've seen more than one salesman take advantage of a person with lesser knowledge or expertise. This is not what I consider ethical, professional or right.

I am committed to interacting with my patients and customers as if they are my brother or sister. I'm always challenging my integrity with the question, "If this were a member of my family, would I recommend this procedure? Am I presenting the best possible solution and filling their true need?"

Focusing on these questions helps me to be more assertive, especially if a patient doesn't understand how important the decision can be in that moment. I've actually said, "If you were my sister or my brother or my father, I would have you do this." I tell them this is for their benefit, not for mine.

I've told people, "I'm not doing this because I'm trying to charge you a fee, I'm trying to help you. I want to help you get something better than what you have." Being assertive isn't uncomfortable for the customer or salesperson when done from a place of integrity and support.

People who have a problem with sales or are afraid of sales don't look at the benefit they create for their customers. They only see it as taking rather than giving. If you really believe in what you are doing, you recognize the sale is a contribution to your customer.

We have an obligation to help our customers say yes to what they want or need when it benefits them and we know we are providing value and service to them. We also have an obligation to let them know when they shouldn't make a purchase if we believe it is not in their best interest.

Our responsibility is to help them make the best decision once we have established value or perceived value.

GET HELP FROM EXPERTS (MENTORS)

Success is not a solo journey. To succeed you need to let others help you improve your business and your life. There are many ways to accomplish this. One is through a relationship with a mentor. I firmly believe you have to take the time to be mentored. There also comes a time you must be willing to share your knowledge by being a mentor.

Being mentored is one of the greatest events that has happened to me. I have had many mentors in my career. Without a doubt, Charlie Schaivo has been my primary and most influential mentor.

However, Charlie didn't teach me everything. What he could not teach he led me to. Charlie is a very smart man. He knew what he could do to influence me and he knew when I needed the expertise of others. He would lead me to courses and to people who could teach me what he could not.

Charlie pointed me towards the DiSC® Profile. As you

read in a previous chapter, learning the DiSC® profile system was one of the most important shifts in business and consciousness I have had in my life. It has helped me immensely in both business and personal relationship building.

I spent a full week learning behavior profiles in 1985 just so I could be more successful in my business. Little did I realize that it would also impact my personal life. I also took a two-day course on Adventures in Attitudes® a couple of years later through Charlie. From there he encouraged me to take more courses in sales, marketing, success, and leadership. All these course have little or nothing to do with dentistry, but everything to do with my ultimate success.

The courses I've taken that were unrelated to dentistry have made me a much more successful dentist than the courses related to building my technical and clinical skills. I am not discounting technical training; it is simply to emphasize that you need a well-rounded education through the guidance of others.

Mentors are essential. You can't pick up a book and read enough to get the accelerated learning that a mentor can provide. It doesn't mean you can't learn these skills on your own, but it's going to take much, much longer. And you will probably never learn at the depth and level you would from a mentor.

In addition to Charlie, there was also Dr. Ciampoli, the dentist I bought my practice from. Even though he had many areas that were antiquated, he taught me a lot about handling people and patients. He was a good mentor for teaching me the importance of being technically competent and honest with patients.

There were many others over the years. Each had something to teach me. Fortunately for me and for all of my patients, I was willing to learn. If there was one thing I would recommend to anyone who wants to be wildly successful, it is to find mentors and learn from them.

Through Charlie I developed a list of mentors/teachers that have served hundreds of thousands of people just like me: Napoleon Hill, Earl Nightingale, Og Mandino, Dennis Whitely, Zig Ziglar, Wayne Dyer, and Mike Vance to name only a few.

I would listen to their tapes until I wore them out and had to get another. I've used the knowledge of seasoned experts as my mentors even though many I have never met in person. I gleaned every bit of wisdom they had to offer. I have found some of the original thought leaders to be so profound I still listen religiously to their material.

Mentorship doesn't have to be a difficult experience. There are very informal as well as formal methods of mentorship. Let's begin with the informal.

Consider the top five people you spend time with the most. Each can be a mentor in his or her own right. To be successful you need to make sure those you associate with most are people that inspire you and lift you up. You must be clear about who you want to spend time with and understand the power they have in your life.

There is an exchange of energy in all relationships. Some people enhance our energy; others can actually deplete our energy. I'm very deliberate in choosing people that increase my energy and fuel my dreams. We may not call one another mentors, but the influence we exert on each other's lives is the same as a mentor/student relationship. I feel so strongly about this I've made efforts in the opposite direction, minimizing relationships with certain people because we weren't on the same track or heading in the same direction.

I look to mentors in both my personal and professional

life. Charlie was a great mentor for my marriage as well as work. Certainly my parents who've been married for over 50 years are incredible mentors when it comes to relationship and marriage.

I have some mentors that I simply examine their life and admire their capacity to live it to the fullest. Take for instance, Euse Mita, the leader of the reflection group in which I am an active member. He is a great example of this kind of person. I have known him for about 25 years and over that time he has mentored me and I sometimes have mentored him. Even though we do not see each other very often, when we do meet and we are together, I walk away a richer person. A brief encounter with Euse can keep me going for days.

There are many forms of mentorship some formal and contractual and some informal existing within the relationship of a friend or family member. As valuable as having a mentor is there will come a time when you are asked to mentor. Seize the opportunity to mentor because the learning never stops! I am currently mentoring a businessman and even though he is learning new things, I am increasing my skills and stay sharp by prepping for our mentoring sessions.

Having the right kind of mentor and noticing who you spend time with leads into the fourth and fifth necessary components for success: *Control Your Thoughts* and *Create Balance in Your Life*. Because the fourth and fifth parts are so important, I have devoted an entire chapter to each.

SUCCESS – A FIVE PART FORMULA
SUCCESS SUMMARY

1. Business Success and Life Success are not exclusive of each other.
2. To have *TOTAL SUCCESS* you need success in both areas.
3. To have *TOTAL SUCCESS* you need to:
   a. Become an Expert (have a great Product and/or Service)
   b. Develop Sales and Marketing Skills
   c. Get help from Experts (have mentors)
   d. Control your Thoughts
   e. Create Balance in your life
4. You may not be the "best" at what you do, BUT be the best you can be.
5. To be the best in your field requires continued training.
6. The success of your business and the success of your personal life is directly proportional to your ability to sell and market.
7. Our lives revolve around selling a Product, Service or idea.
8. Sales is strategic influence, not manipulation.
9. Develop a 'U' Attitude.
10. Always have the customer's interests foremost and have integrity and honesty in your sales process.
11. Sales and Marketing are skills that need to be learned. Very few people are "natural born" sales or marketing people.

12. You need people — mentors — to teach you what you do not know.

13. Find successful people and study their behavior.

14. Mentors can be living or dead.

15. Pay people to teach you what you do not know.

CHAPTER 9

You Are What You Think

I learned a long, long time ago that thoughts control actions and actions are the master of creation in our lives. Actions control the balance of your life whether it is in work, in your relationships, your physical being or your spiritual being. If you can't control your actions, you can't control your balance. If you can't control your balance, it is difficult to control your thoughts.

Thousands of books have been written on the power of thoughts and specific ways to discipline our mind. As advanced as we are in today's world it is still a challenge for most of us to control our thoughts in a way that leads to great success and happiness.

If you don't have control of your thoughts it is very difficult to have any sense of control in your life. Thoughts can be mischievous creatures or wonderful tools for creating success in all areas of life. Controlling our thoughts can lead to results we have only dreamed of. On the flip side, the inability to control our thoughts can lead to nightmares we cannot awaken from.

Even though I may not have been fully aware of it early on, I believe intuitively I've always known the importance of thinking the right way and having a good attitude. I didn't know as much about it in the beginning of my career as I do now, but I knew it had a bearing and an affect.

Charlie insisted I listen to and read the works of many powerful thought leaders; Earl Nightingale's *Lead the Field* and *The Strangest Secret*; Zig Ziglar's *How to Stay Motivated* and *See You at the Top*; Denis Waitley's *The Psychology of a Winner*; Napolian Hill's *Think and Grow Rich*; Og Mandino's *The Greatest Salesman in the World*; Brian Tracy's *The Psychology of Achievement*; James Allen's *As a Man Thinketh* and many others. These men and their works taught me ideas and skills I'd never learned in dental school yet desperately needed in life. I came to recognize that success was about more than money and true happiness required more than a successful business.

Charlie always talked about how powerful attitude is; he still talks like this in his late eighties. What is amazing about Charlie is he is one of the most contented people I know. He doesn't use his age as an excuse to not enjoy life every single day.

He taught me that in order to be successful I needed a positive attitude in every aspect of my life. He understood the deep connection between attitude, thoughts and results. He taught me that the workings of our unconscious mind does not require our understanding; it simply works with or without our direction.

Just like our respiratory system, our mind works without

orchestration, but unlike breathing, we can make choices as to what we allow in and what we do not. We have the ability to choose our thoughts as well as our emotions and craft our lives. I've always loved the quote that says this so well:

"The greatest discovery of my generation is that a human being can alter his life by altering his attitudes of mind."
William James (1842 – 1910)

Although this sounds like something out of many of the new book releases that have recently become so popular, William James was an original thinker in and between the disciplines of physiology, psychology and philosophy from the 19th century.

Between all of Charlie's teachings and the countless books, tapes, seminars and trainings I have taken, I had a deep understanding of the importance of a positive attitude and thinking.

A few years ago, I read the book *Blink; The Power of Thinking Without Thinking*, by Malcolm Gladwell. Mr. Gladwell's writings further piqued my interest in the science behind what the unconscious does and how it impacts our behavior. He cited several examples of how the unconscious controls not only behavior but also physiology. He clearly defines the power of the unconscious leaving no doubt as to who is running the show.

Mr. Gladwell offers multiple examples of the control our unconscious has over us if left undirected. He clears a well-defined path between the workings of the unconscious mind and the body. Thoughts have a definite behavioral and physiological impact.

Between the book *Blink* and various courses I'd taken, as

well as coaching from my past mentors, it really hit home. I was now certain I simply couldn't waiver from choosing my thoughts.

In the past, I had occasion to have a negative attitude and at times almost enjoyed it. When I say I enjoyed it, I mean my negative attitude gave me an "out" and excuses for my life not working. Taking control of my thoughts eliminated the excuses; slamming the door gave me no way out. When you control your thoughts and ultimately your emotions, you are running the show and that knowledge drives home the point, good or bad, you are the director of your life.

I went from a place of, "Okay, maybe this works," to "There is no doubt this works!" The main message I received was this — a thought becomes a thing that manifests in a physical reality. At first, the whole concept of a thought being a thing was hard to wrap my mind around, but with each book I read, each seminar I took, each recording I listened to, I found the concepts to make complete sense.

Our thoughts are like a child in need of discipline to reach its highest potential. Taming our thoughts isn't hard; we only need be schooled in the way of the masters. A wonderful example of just such schooling was when my wife and I attended an accelerated learning course by James Ray called *The Science of Success*. You may recall that James Ray is one of the featured experts in *The Secret*. Before the popularity of *The Secret*, we attended James Ray's course. James is the person who really opened my eyes to some of the science and quantum physics behind thoughts and thinking. Until then, I had evidence that thoughts are powerful things, but not the scientific insights I came to learn.

It was through James Ray's course and further discovery of other teachings that went even deeper into quantum physics and the science of thought that my interest in the power of the subconscious mind reached an all-time high.

During the course James said, "I'm going to teach you how to break through your limiting thoughts. I will do it by teaching you how to break a board."

Having never broken a board in the manner he was going to teach us, I was eager to learn from him and model his strategy. He told us he was committed to showing us we could do it.

"If I passed out boards to everybody and said, 'In four hours I want you to be able to break a board,' there's a good chance that most of you wouldn't be able to do this unless someone shows you how," James said.

This intrigued me because I was now familiar with modeling others from additional studies I had gone through. I knew if someone could do something and they showed you the exact steps, you can replicate the steps and chances are you will also be able to achieve a similar outcome. However, it takes more than just copying the steps. You have to believe that you can achieve the outcome.

James went through the steps one by one. In less than an hour, we were taught what was required mechanically, breathing-wise, physics-wise, as well as the way our hands felt. He showed us the first step, second step, third step. When he showed us the steps, he repeated each one so we heard it continuously.

Within an hour, maybe two, everyone in that room was able to break a board, including my wife. This was no small feat for Anne because she had recently broken her right wrist. She was either going to attempt the board breaking with her left hand or not do it at all. With the way James taught, Anne actually broke the board with her non-dominant hand.

Having everyone, including Anne, break the boards would have been impossible without someone showing us how to control our thoughts and achieve a specific outcome through an accelerated learning process.

What was interesting was that this was a course on thinking; it wasn't a course on breaking boards. James Ray taught me more in two days about thinking than I probably learned in the last 10 or 15 years by reading books.

There are plenty of people who discount how powerful our thoughts are as well as modeling others. These are the people that usually talk about why they can't accomplish what they say they want, rather than exploring reasons why they can. These are often the very same people who criticize successful people and say how lucky the successful ones are. The fact is success leaves evidence. One need only look to see the evidence has been around for centuries.

Most of us think of a thought as intangible because we don't see it. Living in a scientific world that demands visual evidence, it is easy to dismiss the physical reality of a thought because we can't observe it.

We've come to recognize that there is much more that exists outside of our visual field. Simply because we do not see a radio wave doesn't mean it doesn't exist. We've all had the experience or premonition that our thoughts travel and are delivered as intended. We've all thought, "I must give this person a call," only to have the phone ring and on the other end is the person we were going to call.

Did our thoughts pre-empt the call or was it a coincidence? I don't think it was a coincidence or something that happened by accident. We've all shared common thoughts with someone we are close to shouting in amazement, "I was thinking the very same thing!" Another coincidence? I think not. The power of our unconscious is remarkable and a strong ally if we can master our thoughts. Successful people have known this for ages.

SUCCESSFUL THINKING

Thoughts are Things and Thoughts become Things

You've heard me say before success has very little to do with skills and intelligence. It has to do with the way you think, feel and act. Successful people understand their thoughts control their unconscious mind. Their unconscious mind controls their feelings and ultimately their actions. So it makes sense to have thoughts that are related to success and not related to failure. Successful people choose not only their thoughts, but also their emotions. They are clear about the world of attraction as well as the power of frequencies and vibrations. Like attracts like; fear attracts fear; success attracts success!

*Thoughts control our **Unconscious Mind***
*Our **Unconscious Mind** controls our **Feelings** and **Actions***
You must control the thoughts that you put
*into your **Unconscious Mind***

We need to understand the relationship of our thoughts to our feelings and actions. Let's take the negative emotion of anger. When you have a thought that generates the emotion of anger, it creates a certain feeling. That feeling creates a vibration, wave or a frequency, which goes out into the Universe and attracts similar feelings. So if it's a thought with the emotion of anger, it's going to attract that back to you and that creates a certain action and the action gives you the results. The converse or the opposite of it would be the thoughts, say with the emotion of love, creates a certain feeling, vibration or frequency. That goes out into the Universe and attracts a similar feeling. That feeling comes back to you and creates an action and results.

*Thoughts + Emotion produce **Feelings***
Feelings** create vibrations or waves and ultimately **Actions
Actions** = **Results

Think about specific situations you have had. When you are exuding positive emotions, does it not seem as if you are attracting more of the same to yourself? What about negative? When you affirm that a situation just doesn't seem to go right, experiences will show up in your life to support this belief. It's amazing how our subconscious mind is out to prove us right. Regardless of whether we believe situations are good or bad, our experiences will support the belief.

Make no mistake, it's not about sitting in a room thinking positive thoughts and hoping success is going to magically come your way. It's much more than that. Your thoughts must be coupled with the emotions and the feeling. I use this process when setting my goals.

As mentioned throughout this book, my written goals are related to finance, relationships, health, spirituality and speaking. When reviewing my goals, they are preceded and energized by an emotion of excitement, happiness, and gratitude; all those things are important. So I don't just say my goal, I say it with an emotion because that's what gets the results. We're talking about going from a thought, to a feeling, to an action, to a result.

Successful people have a common way of *Thinking* and *Acting*
Change your *Thinking* and you will change your *Results*
You form your *Beliefs* then your *Beliefs form you*
Your *Belief System* is made of your
Thoughts, Feelings and *Actions*

Successful people do have a common way of thinking and acting. The more successful I became the more evident this became. The people I know who made it — and I mean *really* made it — are happy. They are not just successful, they are successful and happy.

Some successful people actually don't think negative thoughts. It's amazing because the more you have a predominant thought process the easier it becomes.

For example, I don't say negative things. When I first began noticing my thoughts and words, it wasn't always easy to shift to a positive state of mind. But over time, it has become a way of life. If I do find I am moving toward negative thoughts and feelings, I now have the tools to shift back to a positive state of mind. It can be something as simple as reminding myself of my goals or reading a book or listening to a CD with positive information. This may seem so simple and elementary. Guess what? *It is!*

You *Become* what you Think about Most
You *Attract* what you Think about Most
Thoughts become *Things*
Don't *Think* about what you Don't Want
Think about what you *Do Want*

It is simply a matter of like attracts like. Successful people's lives are based upon the knowledge that like attracts like and vigilance of thought is necessary for success. They control how they think, so they have greater control as to how they live.

Many people have a belief that successful people are not nice, they don't do nice things and they don't share. It's amazing how misguided that belief is. What's even more amazing is that as long as someone believes that to be true they will deflect their own success rather than attract it.

TOOLS

As much as we know about the power of the unconscious, we all need tools to assist us and support us in our success thinking. There are many tools available, some esoteric, others practical. I encourage students in my training courses and my coaching clients to work with tools that fit their lifestyle and belief systems. I am fairly practical in nature and use tools that are fast and effective. I tell all of my clients the most powerful tool you can use in everyday life is to ask for what you want. Focus on your ultimate goal and experience the feeling of coming from your ideal, not chasing after it.

Unfortunately, many folks are continually focused on what they do not want. This is a dangerous and futile focus! When you make a request of the Universe by asking for what you don't want, that's exactly what you'll get — what you do not want! You must learn to ask for what you want with emotion and on a routine basis. I do this on a daily basis.

GOAL LIST

Every day I focus on my goals and my goal list. Reading about a goal list again may seem redundant, yet it bears repeating. Often we must hear, see and read something multiple times before we really accept it. Writing a goal list is something successful people do.

I was fortunate to learn the power of goals many, many years ago. Not only having goals, but writing them down. Then focusing on the goals by reading them morning and night.

Once I learned the power behind this practice, I have not swayed from it. I am convinced I enjoy the life I do today because of my willingness and commitment to focus on what I want.

What I see happen with people who are not achieving what they want is they may put some effort into goal setting, but they are not consistent with it. They try it for awhile and are then sidetracked by something else. To achieve what you want you must be diligent with this practice.

When I wake up and when I go to bed, I think of each goal I've written down. I feel the emotion of happiness, satisfaction and joy. I experience those emotions from a place of having accomplished my goals, not striving for them. During the day, I have my goal list in my pocket. I can simply touch the list and I know what they are! It's become that big a part of my life.

I've worked with my goal list for so long I no longer need look at it like I did in the beginning. I simply use the paper as a touchstone and reminder to live in the emotion of satisfaction and accomplishment! Each day I touch my pocket, think of the goals listed and experience joy! I know through experience that I've sent a message out to the Universe only to receive the same vibration back in the form of happiness and success. This also helps me to control my thinking.

VISION BOARD

One of my favorite tools to control my thinking is a Vision Board. It is a simple tool that helps me see the end result. Most people are very visual in nature. Because we are so visual, a picture of our success brings what we want into the present as opposed to projecting it into the future.

A Vision Board is a collage of my goals manifest. They've been called many things throughout the years: Treasure Maps, Wish Lists, Attraction Boards. Regardless of what we call them, many successful people have used this simple yet powerful tool to ensure their journey to the end result is a quick one.

A Vision Board helps you establish, visualize and actually reach your most important goals and desired outcomes. Writing down your goals is effective in order to achieve what you want. Combine that with visualization and you become a powerhouse of manifestation!

The process of creating a Vision Board is simple and is really quite fun. You can do the Board development alone or make it a project you and someone close to you both work on.

A quick visit to an arts and crafts store will lend itself to finding most of the initial supplies: paper, scissors, decorative items, glue and even picture frames. Gather up magazines with pictures and phrases that are consistent with the outcome you seek. For example, if you want to manifest a car, get a picture of the car that you can cut out and add to your Vision Board. Let's say you have a certain home in mind. Look for a picture of one that resembles what you have in mind. Cut it out and add it to your board.

As you are putting your images on the Board, feel the feelings of what it will be like when you have the actual item.

What will you say, how will you feel, and what will you hear from others? The more you can immerse yourself into the experience the more powerful the energy behind your manifestation.

For more information on developing a Vision Board, visit www.thesuccesstriangle.com.

Monitor Feelings

Another tool for creating success is to monitor our feelings. I know I can backslide when my thoughts are not positive or my emotions are off. Sometimes I know I've dropped into a negative state simply by the way I interact with people. For example, I can sense my impatience with people in a store or in the bank.

Because thoughts become reality, I know impatience breeds impatience so I'll discipline myself by saying, "I am calm, I have patience through this encounter." In the end, I feel better than I did versus being upset. The situation becomes an enjoyable and happy one rather than a dreaded one.

The fact is I still have to wait in line and do whatever I have to do. I can choose to make it a miserable experience or one that is good for not only me, but also the people I encounter.

We all have the choice of monitoring our feelings. When life isn't going the way you want, you can steam and make negative comments or you can say, "I'm going to just manage this moment and arrive at the result without having the aggravation."

This may seem like a small and inconsequential practice, but it is powerful. Daily aggravations rob us of our wealth and drag us into an ineffective state of mind. How we think about life's situations determines how we feel and ultimately dictates our level of happiness.

As a Catholic, I engage in the practice of Lent, giving something up in the acknowledgement of Jesus' sacrifices. I love sweets so giving them up for Lent was my sacrifice of choice. Instead of succumbing to the negative by saying, "I wish I could eat chocolate; I want to have a candy bar. I can't have a candy bar; I am missing out on the joy of chocolate," I focused on, "I'm eating healthy and this makes me happy," and "I am losing weight because of the way I'm eating and I feel better." Thinking this way really did help stop the cravings. Stopping the cravings allowed me to feel empowered. Feeling empowered created a deeper sense of success.

Our mind is at the core of our power and our mind is in all the cells of our body. Our brain is just a control tower for our mind. We don't need to know why it works, it simply does.

If you can suspend your need for evidence you'll find the world at your feet. If you can surrender to the practice of living from rather than chasing after, you'll find a faith that rewards you through the power of your unconscious mind. I recognize this is tough; we are creatures of habit and control. To focus our thoughts and manage our mind is difficult at best and feels completely unnatural until it becomes a huge part of our everyday process.

FILL YOURSELF FIRST

Charlie loved giving me things to ponder. More than once he would quote the Latin phrase, *"Non dare potes quod non habes,"* which means, *"You cannot give what you do not have."* It is a message about giving to yourself first and then giving to other people, whether it's love, money or happiness.

Before you are in a position to give anything, you must fill yourself first. Fill yourself with proper thoughts — love, gratitude, passion, money and care. Only then can you give these to others.

No one controls your thinking; it is up to you. We have tools, some of us have mentors and all of us crave some kind of muse, but ultimately it is a personal journey. Too many times, we ask others to help us do what we have to do for ourselves. Unless you fill yourself first, you have nothing to give away and you cannot give what you do not have. It is ultimately about loving yourself.

Charlie used to tell me, "When you wake up in the morning, say, "I love myself. I love myself. I love myself." He actually had me practice standing in front of a full-length mirror to affirm my self-love. Granted, in the beginning I didn't quite get it, felt very awkward and even resisted. Yet Charlie never steered me wrong, so I figured if he was recommending it, there was a great reason for this.

If I put half an effort into this practice, as with anything, I received minimal benefit. What I found by doing this with all my heart and soul is I would get into the feeling of joy, love and gratitude. These are very powerful emotions and feelings. Amazing things happen as a result of being in this space. This is a simple practice, but not an easy one.

I enhanced the experience by incorporating this practice at work. Before going in to see a patient, I look in the mirror and say, "I love myself." The key is to really feel this.

It's amazing how much that influenced my experience with the patient. That was another turning point in my life and my business. It all goes back to energy. What we put out we get back tenfold.

It may be easy to talk about giving to ourselves first, but I admit it is not always easy to do. If you were told growing up, "You'll never amount to anything," or "You don't measure up," it's hard to overcome those thoughts. To look in the mirror and say, "I love myself," takes a total reversal of thinking. It's not easy to look in the mirror and say, "I love myself" and mean it. It takes practice, especially for someone experiencing challenges in life. The simple thought of loving yourself creates a certain feeling. That feeling leads to actions and results.

If you follow the steps I have shared with you, you fill yourself first, knowing you are the most important person in your world. You can't give what you don't have. If you fill yourself with thoughts of love, if you fill yourself with thoughts of gratitude, if you fill yourself with thoughts of happiness, you can give them to others in return.

That's why you really have to focus on you. This is not about selfishness or conceit; this is about being "self-centered" in a good way. In this context, self-centered simply means "being in your center."

If you are going to control your thinking, you have to control your life and the way you feel about yourself. YOU are the most important person in your world. Yes, your parents are important, your spouse is important, your children are important, but they are secondary to you because unless you love yourself, you can't be good to those people and give the most you can back to them.

Few are able to control their thinking at all times, but we don't have to struggle all the time either. Much of our struggle is self-induced.

Case in point: In June of 2004, I was in somewhat of a mental funk. I didn't care if my patient or my customer said yes, no or maybe. I had reached a point where I was just going through the motions. If someone wanted what I had to offer, fine. If they didn't want it, that was fine too.

If they wanted something, I'd do it for them, but not with a lot of enthusiasm. I was under less pressure to produce. My children were out of college; I no longer had big expenses. My house was close to being paid off and so many of the goals I strived for I had achieved.

It was the craziest thing. I really thought achieving all the outward stuff would bring me a deeper sense of happiness, but it didn't. I actually found myself not caring and not having the passion I knew I was capable of.

By not having passion and striving for something, it became evident I was losing my edge. For a six month period from June until December, I did not hit my monthly goals. Then in December, I went out to the Las Vegas Institute. I took the occlusion course, a very technical course and not very exciting.

During that four-day course, I associated with dentists who were successful, who liked what they were doing and were making a great income. They were eager and they wanted to improve. They were passionate.

I've been known to tell other dentists, "You can go out to LVI and never take a course. Just associate with the people who are there and come back and improve your practice."

It supports my belief that who you associate with and how you think is key. You have to associate with people with good thinking and a successful orientation. Surround yourself with people who have a balanced life. It is the same with the LVI experience.

After spending my time talking with other dentists, sharing ideas and recommitting to excellence, I came back from that LVI experience all fired up. I thought through my goals and went back to the basics I had been taught decades before.

For the next six months, I hit my goal every month. Then July and August came and I took off two months to go to the shore. For years I have slowed down my practice during the summer to enjoy time with my family at our beach house.

During this particular year, August rolled around and I was going back to LVI to take a two-part course that was six weeks apart. In between that course, I was invited by a dental lab owner in Utah to give a very short presentation to a group of dentists on how to do cosmetic dentistry. This presentation was co-facilitated by Kathleen Gage.

Something amazing happened. During her presentation, Kathleen was talking about some of the very techniques and philosophies Charlie taught me years ago and I had incorporated into my way of thinking. I found myself reaching a new level of excitement.

That evening, Kathleen and I talked for hours about our thoughts, beliefs and actions. I made a commitment right there and then to reach further into my potential then ever before.

After that six week period, I could have jumped through walls. October, November and December ended up being, at that time, the best three months I ever had as a dentist. I actually called the lab I use and said, "What do I have to do to be number one in the lab?"

With that figure in mind, I applied every strategy I knew to achieve the outcome. The ease at which I achieved the number one position with the lab was cause for reflection. Years before I had to put a lot of thought and effort into achieving a specific outcome. Now, since I had a solid foundation for manifestation, it has become almost second nature. That is as long as I utilize the thoughts, beliefs, feelings, and actions formula.

In December of that year, I became the number one producer for the lab. For the following six months, from January until June, I hit my goal every month. My success was not because of skills or increased knowledge or intelligence, it was because of a change in the way I thought, felt and acted. I had learned a valuable lesson.

Life is meant to be **Abundant**
Life is not meant to be a **Struggle**
Inner Happiness powers **Success**

The lesson is that we are meant to have as much happiness as we can handle and embrace. If we put our mind to it, we can achieve just about anything in our life. If we eliminate struggles in our life, we're happier people. Too many times people make life a struggle. Some actually enjoy the struggle; it becomes a way of living. You know who these people are and have had to deal with them.

As I have mentioned, there have been times in my life when I was struggling and enjoyed the struggle, it actually felt good or at least I thought it did. I enjoyed being miserable and making people around me miserable. It was a time of powerlessness; my only satisfaction was having others feel the same sense of powerlessness. I learned much from that period of my life. I learned I wanted to be happy and with that came my willingness to shift my thinking, releasing all struggle. My goal is to be happy.

The unconscious is a hard taskmaster. Clinging tightly to childhood beliefs it can take an intelligent and educated man or woman into the depths of poverty or an average person to the heights of success and fame. One must couple skill, talent and intelligence with an empowering way of thought if success is to be realized.

I know very intelligent people who never experience success or happiness. One man who was at the top of the class in dental school is barely making it in his practice. He hasn't developed the mindset of a successful person. He has not learned to control his thinking.

On the other hand, I know people who didn't finish college and are very successful because they know how to think and act and they control the way they feel.

I equate what I have shared with you about *Control Your Thoughts* to a golf lesson. Assume you've paid a pro to give you a lesson. The pro says, "Here's what I want you to do: I want you to take the stance, do this type of take-away, back swing and come down. As soon as the club gets near the ball, I want you to close your eyes and hit the ball. Then open your eyes and see where the ball goes."

If every time you did this the ball went straight and long, do you think you'd close your eyes at the point of impact? Of course you would, even though it makes no sense at all. That's what I'm asking people to do — to close their eyes. You don't have to see it; you don't have to understand; *you just have to believe it*. If what you're currently doing is not working, you have nothing to lose and only your dreams to gain.

Many a master has left us with thoughts and benchmarks to assist us on our path to success. Every successful person has mastered their thoughts and immersed themselves in the knowledge and wisdom of others. I've used certain principles as guidelines for controlling my thoughts and living my dream.

Through Charlie and all the inspirational and success coach greats, I came to understand the impact of my thoughts, emotions, feelings and actions on my life. As time went on, I came to realize the importance of my mental and emotional environment. It became crystal clear I had control of my future, good or bad.

Control Your Thoughts
Success Summary

1. Learn and read as much as possible on thinking, controlling your thoughts and managing your attitude.
2. Have a conscious awareness of your thoughts and the impact they have on your unconscious, your actions and results in life.
3. Avoid contact and relationships with people who have negative thinking, are not going where you are going, or who are just not happy people.
4. *Thoughts* are *Things* and *Thoughts* become *Things*.
5. Success has very little to do with *Skills*.
   Success has very little to do with *Intelligence*.
   Success comes from your *Thoughts* — *Feelings* — *Actions*.
6. *Thoughts* control our Unconscious Mind.
   Our Unconscious Mind controls our *Feelings* and our *Actions*.
   You must control the thoughts that you put into your Unconscious Mind.

7. *Thoughts* + *Emotion* produce *Feelings*
   Feelings create vibrations or waves and ultimately
   Actions
   Actions = *Results*
8. Successful people have a common way of *Thinking* and *Acting*.
   Change your *Thinking* and you will change your *Results*.
   Form your *Beliefs* then your *Beliefs* form you
   Your *Belief System* is made up of your *Thoughts*, *Feelings* and *Actions*.
9. You become what you think about most and you *Attract* what you think about most.
10. Think about **what you want**, not what you don't want.
11. Life is meant to be *Abundant*. Don't focus on lack or scarcity and what you do not have.
12. Life is not meant to be a *Struggle*. *Inner Happiness* powers *Success*.

My goal for you with this chapter was to show you how important your thoughts are to your success. Although many people have heard this repeatedly and in countless ways, the missing link is in knowing how to create balance in order to be of clear mind, heart and spirit to maintain positive thoughts. In the next chapter, you will learn a formula my mentor taught me decades ago that is so important to my success, I use it to this day. *The Circle of Balance* is an easy to use process that immediately indicates areas you may need to put attention on in order to have a high level of balance both professionally and personally.

CHAPTER 10

The Circle of Balance

One of Charlie's main messages to me was about the importance of balance. He was convinced that without balance achieving *TOTAL SUCCESS* was all but impossible. Charlie had a very unique way of introducing the concept of balance to someone. It was with *The Circle of Balance*.

When Charlie first shared *The Circle of Balance* with me over 30 years ago, I didn't understand it like I do today. What I thought was balance at 20 years old is very different from what I know balance to be in my mid-50's. Age is a great teacher for all of us if we are willing to pay attention. Each passing day I have a clearer and clearer understanding of what balance means and how it impacts every aspect of my life.

Balance may be a misnomer; minimally it is a verb not a noun. To maintain balance one is always adjusting, never stationary and never in the perfect place at the perfect time. I've benefitted so much from using *The Circle of Balance* I offer it to my clients, mentees, family and friends.

I shared *The Circle of Balance* with both of my children when they went away to college because I think that's when obvious ties are cut from child to parent and there is a lot of temptation to live an unbalanced life.

THE CIRCLE OF BALANCE

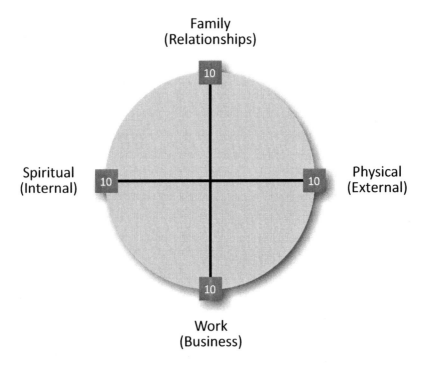

Family
(Relationships)

Spiritual
(Internal)

Physical
(External)

Work
(Business)

Not everybody, including myself, has balance at all times. By giving attention to four main areas in your life, you can stay closer to steadiness on a consistent basis than if you give it no attention at all.

The reality is you can't correct something you don't understand or think about. As simple as it may seem many people struggle to balance their life and live in true happiness.

Here's how it works. The center of the circle is zero with the outside being ten. You have family on the top, which is balanced by work on the bottom. On the right-hand side of the circle is the physical or external being, balanced by the spiritual or internal being.

We spend much of our life at work. Relationships are another area we spend much of our time. The physical part of our external body has two components: health and fitness. Health comes before fitness. You cannot be unhealthy *and* fit. You do not have to become an exercise fanatic, but you do need a certain degree of health in your life to be effective with family and work.

If you don't have family or personal relationships, work and your physical health in order, it's very difficult to have your spiritual life in order.

One of my greatest goals in life is to be happy. It's hard to be happy when you're out of balance or deficient in any area of your life. I'm not sure I completely understood the need for happiness in my life until recently.

Regardless of how much we do to stay in balance, I think we should recognize we're always in a state of flux. The state of flux allows for necessary adjustments that permit growth and expansion in our lives.

For example, on a scale of 1 to 10, 10 being the best a relationship can be, I may often find myself between an eight and nine. There was a time I was at a two or three before I really paid attention to the wisdom Charlie taught me with *The Circle of Balance.* Now that I have a vision of where I strive to be, I adjust my thoughts, actions and beliefs in all areas of my life in order to get closer to a ten on a consistent basis.

There are times I may slip a little in the areas of work, health or fitness and I'm not always at a 10. The issue is not that I'm less than a ten, it is "Am I willing to recommit to my happiness? Am I willing to do what it takes to be the kind of person I want to be?"

Life is about choices and commitments. Our choices and commitments either move us closer to happiness or further away. Every day I have the opportunity to choose the actions I take to move me closer to the person I want to be.

Happiness is holistic; it encompasses so much in life. Take money for example. Many people think money is the foundation for happiness. Money *is* an important part of being happy, but it is not the source of happiness.

Usually people with very little material abundance say money can't bring you happiness. The truth is money allows you the freedom to do things that are enjoyable. In and of itself, money is not the source of happiness, but a tool for creating experiences that we would not be able to have without having money at our disposal. Having and knowing how to use the energy of money is an aspect of happiness and balance.

We create our own happiness by controlling our thoughts, mastering our craft, nurturing our relationships, taking time for the spiritual as well as the physical. We create our own happiness by recognizing every breath is a gift and every moment unique.

Each day I live a life of choice. I'm lucky enough to decide what I want to do, how I want to think, how I want to serve. Each day I am offered limitless moments of happiness that I need only recognize and receive.

I am often asked what I believe has contributed the most to my success. Without a doubt, it has been the ability to keep relative balance in various areas of my life.

Living a balanced life is a challenge for many people. Often, due to the pressures and demands of everyday living, we are tempted to live life as if tomorrow will never come. When life is out of balance it is natural to assume one aspect of life is more important than another. We may live with the belief that focusing attention on one area of life while neglecting the others will never catch up with us. For years, this was true for me until I learned how to use this simple tool.

In essence, *The Circle of Balance* is a tool that can be used by virtually anyone to determine what is working in his or her life and what isn't. With Charlie's guidance, I began to assess my life. Through ongoing assessment, I have been able to achieve a very deep meaning to my life.

As I mentioned, I found myself to be incredibly out of balance in my early career. This is common with people who want to achieve success. Often, overindulgence in work is the ultimate temptation as we strive to achieve success in our life. We convince ourselves hours upon hours of work are justified as acceptable; after all work holds the possibility of future riches.

A lot of sacrifice here for financial gain there is a natural and oh, so tempting way to live. As tempting as it is, an extreme focus in one direction will eventually blind us to the other dimensions of life. We can neglect those areas of life until they demand our attention in a dramatic and often unpleasant way.

Using *The Circle of Balance* brings the basic components of life into focus. *The Circle of Balance* is deceptively simple yet profoundly powerful when used as a touchstone for a successful life.

THE FOUR ELEMENTS OF
THE CIRCLE OF BALANCE

There are four elements in *The Circle of Balance*: Work, Family, Physical and Spiritual. Let's take a look at each element in greater detail.

WORK

In the greatest sense of the word, work can be a major contribution on our part. A balanced life demands an outlet for contribution and creativity. Our work life can hold our passion, be a source of satisfaction and — for a lucky few — spiritual bliss. However, it can also detract from life's pleasures if it controls your existence or is all you live for.

Whether you own your business or are employed within an organization, work is a very creative process. In truth, you have a choice as to *when* you work and *how much* you work. You can work too much or too little. You can overachieve, underachieve or take yourself out of the game completely.

If you work too little, you may not produce enough money or have enough income to be happy. Your relationships may suffer because you're not providing for your family or doing your fair share. On the other hand, you may be working too much, whereby you're hurting your relationships. In both cases, you're hurting yourself. Unfortunately, work is a very acceptable escape in our culture. An imbalance at work is guaranteed to produce an imbalance in life.

FAMILY

The term "Family" includes your immediate family as well as extended family; the people you associate with on a very close basis, your relationships. Our family is our community. Without family, life can be meaningless and accomplishments empty in the absence of human touch and connection. Ultimately, love is everything and loving relationships require self-love.

Not a day goes by that we aren't impacted by the nature of our relationships. It can be difficult to maintain healthy and vital relationships. If we are not responsible in our personal relationships, it affects us in two ways; it affects how we feel about ourselves and it also affects our work. It is unrealistic to assume our personal life does not influence our work life. In essence, you bring your relationships to work.

For example, if you are unable to stay in a relationship or you cheat on your spouse or partner, I think this affects your family *and* your work life. If your children are involved in drugs, alcohol, being arrested or have personal turmoil, this will definitely affect your personal and family life. It will also affect your business life.

Human beings are very sensitive to energies. Ask any staff member and they'll be able to tell you in-depth details about the boss' life. We are seen at work within the context of our relationships. Relationships offer many lessons and some hard learned. It is easy to leave and start again only to find a cycle of blame and punishment substituted for growth and true intimacy. A balanced life calls for deep human contact. Just as an infant will not thrive without human touch, we suffer the same sensory deprivation.

PHYSICAL

The physical holds two components: health and fitness. Health being the way you treat your body; the way you eat, drink, how much sleep you get, the care you take of yourself, etc. Fitness is what you do to maintain or improve your health. Fitness includes movement, exercise and the vitalization of our energy. Health must precede fitness.

Health and fitness are two components of our physical being. It is obvious by the age-old statement, "If you have your health, you have everything," that a strong and vibrant body is a primary element to a happy and successful life. Health relates to our general well-being: whether we're sick or not, the way we eat, our diet, and our habits. If we're lucky enough to have the option to choose health it is a powerful and empowering choice. There isn't an area of your life that is not impacted by your health.

Our eating, drinking and drug use habits all have an impact on our relationships, our families and the way we behave at work. We can choose to overindulge in any area or apply moderation in order to maintain a balanced life.

It's hard to be fit if you're not healthy, or at least have a degree of health. That's why health precedes fitness. Our national struggle with obesity is a perfect example of the connection between health and fitness.

Fitness is readily available to most of the population but it requires a degree of commitment. As your health and fitness improves the ability to be energized at work and in relationships improve. It is all connected.

SPIRITUAL

When the three areas of your life; work, relationships, and health; are not above a five or six on a scale of one to ten, it's pretty hard to have a sense of spirituality. When you're in relationships that are failing, work is unsatisfying or unsuccessful, and you're living in a body that has been neglected it is difficult to see the spiritual side of life.

To achieve balance and spirituality it is necessary to take time to nurture and connect with something beyond ourselves. As previously mentioned, I believe and know in my heart spirituality encompasses many things. Everyone has his or her own definition of what it is. For me it is supported by a church and a God, but it includes other things as well.

Spirituality is as different and diverse as there are people on the planet. For many people, it is not necessarily always a church and a God. Spirituality can include quiet time, reflection and meditation and an understanding of your inner person or spirit. You see, I believe God is in all of us.

The quiet time allows us to consider the impact we have on our family and relationships, our health, what our roles and responsibilities are and how essential our actions are. Evaluating these areas of your life will keep your spiritual life in order.

The Circle of Balance is designed to ultimately achieve a ten in all areas. This is the goal, but is not always attainable. Balance comes from keeping each area in focus in order to put effort into all aspects of our life.

These are the principles behind *The Circle of Balance*. As you will read in the next chapter, once Charlie introduced me to the power behind this amazing tool, my life went through a drastic change. For me, my thoughts and perception had forever been shifted.

To access your own downloadable *Circle of Balance*, visit www.thesuccesstriangle.com.

THE CIRCLE OF BALANCE
SUCCESS SUMMARY

1. The four areas that require balance are Work, Family, Physical, and Spiritual.
2. We are usually never in balance in all areas at all times.
3. It is hard to be happy when you are out of balance; balance leads to happiness.
4. Your Work (business), Family (relationships) and Physical (external, health) all affect each other. It is all connected.
5. It is difficult to have a Spiritual component (inner peace) when the other three areas of our life are not in balance.
6. A commitment is needed in all four areas of balance or balance will not happen.
7. We can work too much or too little. Both can hurt our family and our physical being. An imbalance at work is guaranteed to produce an imbalance in life.
8. Relationships are important for happiness. An imbalance in Family (relationships) can affect your work and physical being.
9. Physical has two components: health and fitness.
10. Health precedes fitness.
11. As your health and fitness improve, the ability to be

energized at work and in relationships improve.

12. For some Spirituality is a church and a God, for others it is an inner peace.

13. Spirituality can include energy, quiet time, reflection and meaning and an understanding of your inner person or spirit.

14. Evaluating the various areas of your life will keep your spiritual life in order.

CHAPTER 11

Balance — A Requirement for TOTAL SUCCESS

By the time I was in my late twenties, I really felt as if I had arrived. I was making great money, driving a fancy car and living in a big house. Everything I based success on, I had. The harsh reality was, my life was in turmoil. Although I had a level of success, I didn't have *TOTAL SUCCESS*.

It's the same with my friends who make millions and millions of dollars annually. They make more than I'll make in a lifetime and yet they don't have what I now understand to be *TOTAL SUCCESS*. They only have *professional* success.

Their main focus is business. They have difficulty in relationships, failed marriages, problem children, they misuse their authority and power and they eat and drink to excess. Their life is in turmoil and their lifestyle is killing them. I don't know how to assess another's spiritual well-being, but I think that it's hard to have inner-peace when your life is in turmoil. My experience has shown me a successful life is more than a successful business.

This was a lesson hard learned. By the time I had "arrived" I was working way too much; 60 to 70 hours a week, sometimes more. I'd work until ten o'clock on Friday nights and often be in my office on weekends. I was driven to be successful in my business.

As I mentioned earlier, the first year out of dental school I made $50,000. This was under very poor conditions. Even though this was a lot of money by most people's standards, my goal was to make $100,000 the second year. In 1978, that was a ton of money and I pulled out all the stops in order to reach that goal. By today's standards that would be $300,000 - $400,000 a year.

I was driven to produce. Nothing was going to stop me. I did what I needed to do continually for the next couple of years. I had arrived, so I thought. I was 29 years old. I had a five-bedroom house on a 1-acre lot, a Mercedes-Benz, and my life looked great — from the outside.

What wasn't apparent to a casual observer was I also had a wife and children I never saw, or saw very little. Even though I was doing what I thought a good husband should do, my wife was very upset. She was doing everything with the kids and I was not there to help and support her on that level.

Anne was so upset, I would come home at night and she would scream at me and say, "You're not here; you're not helping. I can't go on like this!" I found myself making many promises like, "I'm only going to do this for a little while, it's going to get better, and I'm going to change." A year would go by and I wouldn't change; I continued to be driven to make the money to prove I was successful.

Where I grew up, not many of my friends went to college. The fact that I became a dentist was a step above. I was hell-bent on showing people that it doesn't matter where you start, you can make something of yourself. I would constantly affirm, "I came from a working class neighborhood; I am now successful and make enough money to buy whatever I want."

What was important at the time was to make enough money to show people I was successful. At that point in my life, it was more about showing them I was successful than living a successful life. The one way I could do it was to make a lot of money.

People would say, "Wow. You've made it!" That meant a lot to me! Little did I realize all my focus on business and money was putting my life completely out of balance.

I suppose if I would have paid attention to what my wife was saying and how I was feeling I would have known how out of balance I was.

It wasn't until 1983 that I began to recognize the need for balance. Work was a major disruption in my life even though it was giving me my perceived success. Although I had been ignoring it for a long time, there was now no denying that I needed to do what I could to have a balanced life.

First, I took steps to fix my business. As my business improved, I started paying consultants to help me learn how to run my business more efficiently. It was through these business improvements I was able to take more time with my family. This allowed me to be home with my family more and focus on my physical balance. This was pivotal in improving my relationship with my wife and children and my health.

My wife is a great mother and a wonderful spouse for

hanging in there until I was present and accounted for on the home front. Most striking to me was that as I came into a kind of physical and professional balance, my marriage came into balance as well. This then opened up the part of my life that was lacking, the spiritual inner component.

It was during that time Charlie introduced me to a way of life that would forever change me. Charlie was an advocate of living a very balanced life and he made no qualms about the importance of this. He said, "The more balanced your life becomes, the more success you can create. The more balance you have the more you will realize what you are capable of and how connected everything is."

By now I was keenly aware that all aspects of my life were connected at a deep level. I could no longer address one area without addressing another. Once I knew this, I could no longer go back to my old way of thinking, acting and believing. Everything was shifting.

I came to realize my wife and family deserved as much attention as my business. It was during that time I created goals concerning my family relationships. I wanted and needed to be a contributor.

One of my goals was to be the best husband I could be. With this as my focus, a shift began. Just the fact I had a focus on improvement the changes began.

I made a conscious effort to say something positive about my wife everyday. Not necessarily big things, but things like, "Honey, you're the best. You look beautiful today. I appreciate all that you do." The key was to convey my feelings with sincerity, not just to hear myself talk.

By running my business better and having systems in place at work, I had more time to share with my family and enjoy time with my wife. I made a conscious effort to do little things like help around the house. Even though I was running a business, making this kind of a change made a huge difference. I would catch myself saying things like, "Can I help you do anything?" and "Why don't you let me get that for you?"

The most amazing thing began to happen. I found I was feeling more love for my wife than I ever had. I began focusing on what I love and appreciate about my wife. I found the more I focused, the more desire I had to be a contributing husband and the better my life became. It became very apparent positive business changes were having a positive effect on my personal life.

It was the same with my health. As my business improved, I was now putting effort into my physical well-being. The healthier I became, the better my personal relationships became and the better I performed in my business. I was now experiencing what Charlie had often talked about: balance in all areas of my life.

I was gaining an insider's view that what we focus on increases. It is one of the most basic principles of success, yet one that is the most underutilized.

Creating balance isn't a big secret. It's really about doing the very basics. Actually, it's more about doing the basic stuff than making massive change all at once.

Balance includes our thoughts and goes back to controlled thinking and focus. To create balance you have to watch your thought process and what you ask for.

I use my thinking to support my relationships, my health, my finances and my spirituality. For example, around my relationship with my wife, I will repeat to myself, "I love being with my wife and I am happy to be with her."

It goes back to the saying, "Energy flows where your attention goes." So if my attention is on the positive, energy flows there. I fill my mind and heart with the positive and don't let thoughts of conflict, fear or lack rob my peace.

One of the biggest tools that has helped the balance in my marriage is the use of DiSC® Classic. My wife's dominant behavior pattern is different from mine, therefore I know we're going to have different wants and desires. Sometimes I have to concede to her wants and desires if I truly want a happy relationship.

I've learned not to fight about insignificant things. As strange as that sounds, I just don't fight anymore. Being somewhat of a hotheaded Italian, I've been known to say the wrong thing too quickly. I've just learned not to do this anymore in my marriage. It isn't worth the imbalance it creates. I now know I can choose what I say and what I do. I also know how much significance or insignificance I place on anything is up to me.

I've learned a balanced life requires discipline and attention. In order to thrive in my relationship with my wife, I have to bring the same discipline to our marriage that I've brought to my business. There is a relationship between work and family that balance each other. One supports the other.

Although it may sound as though my discipline is to hold my tongue, this is not so. My discipline is to see love where there could be conflict, peace where at one time there was fear and balance even when the circle is a little out of kilter. In the scheme of things, I don't win by winning an argument. I'm not happier when we argue.

My work relationships demand the same balance. My team and the other dentists in the office and I know each other's behavior style. We've all taken the DiSC® Classic profile so we have a deep understanding and respect for the differences that create our team and our partnership.

We think before we talk. We understand when someone says or does certain things that may be irritating, they're probably not doing it to aggravate us. They simply have a different style.

A huge part for me in creating balance is I've given up the thought of self-importance. I have come to recognize that many times someone's actions are just a part of his or her behavioral style and is not a reflection on me. The objective is to value everyone and make the situation better. Relationships at home and work affect your business success.

My desire for a more balanced life began to shift around the time I was trying to change the business. Strange things happen when you work 70 or 80 hours a week. You go to work, come home, eat, and sleep. You wake up and do the same thing the next day. And the next. And the next...

I would literally come home, eat a regular meal at ten o'clock, have a beer or two, and go to bed. Without any type of physical activity, I put weight on. After awhile, I got a Hiatal hernia, the type of hernia where the stomach pushes up through a hole in the diaphragm muscle. It is very painful. I had chest pains every time I'd lie down. I wasn't very old and my body was becoming that of an old man.

I had to change my eating habits because of the hernia, the weight gain, the lack of energy and just not feeling good overall. I turned things around by minimizing my consumption of alcohol, reducing my meat intake and making a commitment to participate in a healthy diet for a period of a year.

It was during this time I decided I wanted to play tennis

again. Before I could play, I needed to get in better shape. I decided the first thing I would do is run a couple miles at the local track.

I struggled the first time on the track. Shocked and disgusted, I realized I was 30 years old and I couldn't even run a mile. Something happened in that moment. I vowed to get in top physical shape from that point forward.

I said to myself and to my wife, "I am going to run four days a week, rain or shine, no matter what, and eat a healthy diet." To this day, over 25 years later, I have kept the commitment.

I realized I had been shortchanging others by the choices I had made up to that point. A part of me acknowledged it wasn't fair to have a low energy level when I'd go to work. I knew my family would eventually suffer if my health were less than the best I could achieve. With a commitment to running and improving my health, I could keep my commitments to work and play harder on the weekends.

For the past 25 years, the number of times that I have not run four days a week is less than ten, and that's because of matters that were out of my control. The number of times I haven't run because I didn't feel like it is zero. I have never gone to the door and said, "Well, it's cold, it's raining, it's snowing... I don't feel like running today."

I've run with a fever, I've run and thrown up, I've run in blizzards. I've run in rain, I've run when it is hot. I've run because it's my day to run. To this day my wife says, "I know you're crazy going out there," and I say, "Yeah, I know, but I'm going to do it anyway," and I do it. I know this is not for everybody. This is simply the degree of commitment I've dedicated to my health and fitness.

The bottom line is that commitment is required in all areas of life. A commitment to your business, your relationships, your physical and spiritual being. I never lie about my commitments. When you lie about your commitments the first time, it makes the second time much easier, and the third time easier yet. Soon there is no commitment, then there's no structure, and eventually you are out of balance. When you lie to yourself it impacts your self-worth and value.

A strange thing happened when recapturing my balance; the physical improvement came first, then business started to get better. That's when my relationships started to get better. My relationships improved because I was able to spend more quality time with my wife and children. This did not happen in a matter of weeks; this took a period of four to five years to occur. In an instant gratification world, it is important for people to realize success takes time. Time takes commitment and commitment takes integrity to one's self. It is like the old saying goes, *To Thine Own Self Be True*.

As my physical life, relationships and business were balancing out, the strangest thing began to happen. I found my desire for a more balanced spiritual life begin to take hold.

In 1985, Charlie Schaivo introduced me to yet one more instrument that would have a profound impact on my life. Charlie said to me, "Joe, why don't you come along on this retreat to Malvern?" Not knowing what Malvern was or what to expect, I avoided making the commitment to go, but eventually I did go, because by now I really trusted Charlie's guidance.

With the decision to go to Malvern, little did I know what an incredible experience awaited me and that my life would change forever.

Malvern is a Christian retreat that happens to be

Catholic. You don't have to be Catholic to participate. It's a semi-structured weekend with religious services, quiet time, reflection time, meditation and prayer. They have a retreat master who gives various talks throughout the weekend based on a specific theme.

Malvern was so amazing I vowed to attend every year without ever allowing any excuses. My first retreat at Malvern so moved me that when I came home from the weekend I told Charlie, "If I ever tell you I can't go to Malvern, tell me I'm a liar. There will never be a reason why I can't go."

The time I invested at Malvern made me realize I needed a period at least once a year to have quiet time; to look back over the previous year and reflect. Until I really participated in quiet time, I didn't realize how much I craved it.

The Malvern Retreat is held during the Father's Day weekend. My friends and family know that this is my weekend. Actually, I passed on Charlie's legacy to my son. He's been coming since he was 15, and like me, attends every year without fail.

We spend the weekend together as father and son. The retreat provides us with quality time, a time to be together, and a time to talk together. It is about connection, reflection, and silence.

Our lives are bombarded with noise, both internal and external. Cell phones, iPods, computers, e-mails, faxes; you name it, we have it and it is only going to increase.

To consciously take time to reflect is an incredible experience and a tool of balance. Once exposed to the quiet, I recognized how overwhelmed I had actually become.

In addition to Malvern, following Charlie's example, I started to go to church services in the morning. Even though my work schedule often prevented me from staying for the entire church service, I was still able to sit quietly for 15 minutes or so. During that time, I enjoyed the quietness of just sitting there. It didn't matter if there was a priest at the altar or even whether a church service was going on or not; it was simply a time to connect to the quietness.

When I first went deep into my spiritual journey, I was at a crossroads in many areas of my life. As most people do, I often had questions in my life that needed answers. Some of the questions I had were not easy. Some of my questions were business related, some about home, and others about relationships.

With the business, I might be grappling with finances and taking on other dentists or employees. I knew it was important to think through whatever decision I made.

My family issues required I go deep into myself. Sitting in the quiet the answers came to me with grace and at times with ease. The longer I have made quiet time a part of my spiritual foundation, the easier it becomes to receive information from the Divine.

Although for me spirituality is a church, a God, a belief and Divine intervention, it may not be that way for everyone. Even if people don't believe in a God per se, many believe there are energies or forces out there that control the Universe. I think we all need quiet time in today's world. Spirituality is a vehicle to quietness and inner reflection.

I have found that having a time and a place for quiet time in my home and life has enhanced me in ways that often amaze me. In the 25 plus years since beginning my reflection time, I no longer walk into a room and unconsciously turn on the radio or TV. Prior to that time, I would use the noise as a distraction. Noise is a great avoider of reflection. I often say, "You cannot hear when there is noise." Now I consciously work at minimizing the distractions and increasing the quiet time.

Make quiet time to be with yourself and to reflect. If you can't be comfortable taking time to be with yourself, how can you expect others to want to be with you?

The purpose of quiet time isn't just relaxation, there is more to it. It helps with our creativity and problem solving. For example, when your mind goes from the conscious state to the state just prior to sleep, you produce a greater amount of alpha waves. When your mind is producing alpha waves, you're more open to receiving ideas and you're more creative in your thought process.

In fact, Thomas Edison unknowingly would practice thinking in an alpha state. He would sit in the late afternoon with a lead ball in his hand when he was tired and blocked. He'd close his eyes and await a sense of slumber until he would drop the ball. He wanted the ball to wake him before he fell into sleep knowing this level of consciousness would produce good ideas and enhance his creativity when he opened his eyes.

Edison's process is basically a form of a meditation. I know the impact and importance of a meditative state. In essence, it is simply a focused, quiet state. While in dental school, I took a course on transcendental meditation. This was not a part of the dental curriculum, but done independently. I also participated in studies based upon transcendental meditation and how the results of meditation in producing alpha waves compared to progressive relaxation, self-hypnosis and hypnosis. Amazingly, all four states produced increased alpha waves, thus showing that quietness in any of these situations allows you to be more creative and productive. It is not necessary to take courses in any or all of these areas. You can reap the benefits of an alpha state just by developing quietness in your life.

Here is a very simple step virtually anyone can implement to find serenity, peace, and increased creativity. Find a place within your home or your life where you can take 5 to 10 minutes. Sit with your eyes closed. Just sit in a chair for a few minutes. You can concentrate on your breathing, or you can repeat a simple phrase or mantra.

I frequently do this during my lunch break. I close my eyes and repeat a personal mantra. After a mere 10 minutes, I wake up extremely energized. I notice in the quiet I have a greater sense of my own truth; my gut instinct is honed and an intuitive wisdom is developed. Quietness is a simple tool with deep and lasting benefits.

The mantra you repeat can be a word, a phrase or a sound. A mantra usually has a personal meaning attached to it. The most important thing is to simply allow yourself quiet time.

I have also deepened my spiritual practices by participating in a gospel reflection group that meets every Friday morning. I have attended sessions for the last few years with a group of very successful business owners, mostly high-powered men who have a diverse mix of backgrounds, experiences and religions. We connect by way of a gospel reading, which we then relate to daily life and the things we should or could be doing better.

This gospel group has been very revealing. To hear other men, who I admire and respect for what they have accomplished, share their insights is incredible. They know the importance spirituality plays in their life. Their commitment to balance is remarkable. They are a group of men that hold fast to what they know. One of the sayings we have there is, "Once you know, you cannot not know."

This simply means once a truth has been revealed to you, it is difficult to act on an old behavior that is no longer in your best interest or serves your highest good. For example, in our group we have discussions about honesty in business, fidelity in our marriage, and living a life of integrity. Although any one of us could act on a behavior or a moment's temptation, we will likely choose not to. Not because we couldn't get away with something and hide something from others, it is because in our heart we would know we went against the core values we live by.

It goes back to my experience of recognizing what I needed to do to have true balance in my life. Once I became aware, there was no going back.

I'm not sure I could have accomplished all that I have without this concept of spirituality and balance. In the last 5 to 10 years, my balance has been above average. I have a life that that I am proud of and is filled with happiness. I do not say this to impress anyone. I say it to impress upon you that you can create an amazing life with lasting success. It simply takes awareness, willingness and action.

I have had people ask me if I am 100% certain about my concept of God and spirituality. Actually, it doesn't matter if what I believe is true or not. I say this because if I died tonight and I get to wherever I'm going only to find there is no Heaven and no God, I would be satisfied. I'd look back on my life and say, "I'm glad I did it that way, because I was a happier person. I lived my life based on principles that made me happy and made others happy." So I don't live or think this way to reap the benefits of Heaven. I live this way and believe this way because it gives me a quality of life that is truly passionate, joyful and loving.

I know life is fragile; it could fall apart tomorrow, but I'd still have my sense of self and the knowledge to recreate and rebalance this gift we call "life."

I am asked frequently what my "secret" to success is. My secret is not a secret at all; it is simply about balance and awareness. It needn't be difficult and it is available to almost everyone. At times it may not be the easiest thing to achieve, yet the more you strive for it, the easier it becomes.

When we can link our worldly successes with spiritual understanding, we will bridge the great divide of being materially successful and spiritually rich.

First, understand what the four areas of balance are and do a self-assessment using *The Circle of Balance*. After you've assessed your state of balance, create an action plan for improving your work, relationships, and your physical well-being. If you can commit to improving these three areas of your life, the spirituality side of life will come together on its own without a lot of effort and what effort you do put into it will be well worth it.

I have tried to create success in both my business and personal life in order to achieve TOTAL SUCCESS. Success in business alone is incomplete. Given the choice of one of these two areas, I would choose to have a successful personal life.

Understanding of *The Circle of Balance* and taking action to have balance has allowed me the gift of having success both personally and professionally and the ability to achieve TOTAL SUCCESS.

One of the greatest benefits in achieving TOTAL SUCCESS is our ability to share what we have with others. The principle of giving and sharing reaches back through the centuries. It is a spiritual principle that took me some time to really grasp, yet all the most successful people I know subscribe to this principle. In the next chapter I share what it took for me to fully grasp this concept and how pivotal it has been in my life.

BALANCE
SUCCESS SUMMARY

1. *TOTAL SUCCESS* requires more than a successful business and a great income.
2. Success in your personal life is more important than success in your business.
3. Pay people to get your work (business) to run more efficiently.
4. As work and physical worlds come into balance, family life comes into balance as well.
5. The more balanced your life becomes, the more success you can create.
6. As your physical life, relationships and business balance out, you find the desire for more of a spiritual component in your life.
7. We need some quiet time and reflection time in our day. Our lives are bombarded by noise.
8. It is hard to hear when there is noise.
9. Find a place in your home or work where you can experience quiet.
10. Quiet opens the mind.
11. To move towards a 10 in all four areas requires a commitment to action.
12. Once you lie to yourself about a commitment, the second and third time the lie becomes easier and

soon there is no commitment.

13. *TOTAL SUCCESS* requires a successful business and personal life.

14. *The Circle of Balance* can guide you to *TOTAL SUCCESS*.

CHAPTER 12

The Million-Dollar Letter

One of the most rewarding aspects of having achieved the level of success I now enjoy is my ability to make financial contributions to causes I believe in. I am also in a position to contribute my services when I feel called to do so.

My mother-in-law taught me about the importance of giving. Anne's mom is one of the smartest people I know. Back when Anne and I didn't have a lot to give, Mom would say, "You have to be willing to give. Give to your church, give to your community and give to others."

Even though it was a real stretch and at times emotionally painful, I found her words to be true. The more I was willing to give, and give freely, to the places I felt called to give to, the more I received. Not just tenfold, but twenty, thirty, even a hundred fold.

We live in a world where people are constantly asked for money. If you have a lot of money, giving to others is pretty easy to do. If you don't, it's very difficult. My philosophy is to give to the people I think are most deserving. I have certain causes I contribute to: I give to our church and the Malvern Retreat. I've learned you always get back what you give and at times even more.

I've found I had to pick specific causes because it is too difficult to give to all of them. Always thinking of donations in terms of dollars, it wasn't until recently I understood the value of contributing one's service versus giving one's dollars. Many businesses offer discounted services here and there, but sometimes you have to do something on a large scale to have a real impact.

As a successful dental practice, we're constantly bombarded for contributions to different causes and organizations. We do have a charitable giving budget and we do contribute to local children's groups, sports groups, and other types of organizations. We also have big hearts and we write off a fair amount of dentistry.

Our team knows we're profitable and they know we're on the higher end of the fee scale. With that kind of success there is a sense of empathy for people who need our services but simply can't afford them.

If someone is in trouble and we really believe we can help, we'll write off their balance or we'll give them a break. If we did two fillings, we might charge them for one. That's just the human side of what we do. We are sensitive to life's challenges and if someone is really having a hard time financially, we do what we can to help. Although I *thought* I was a very giving person, it wasn't until I met Jackie Restuccia that my perspective on giving and receiving changed.

I am convinced meeting Jackie was no accident. Our paths were meant to cross. Permit me to explain.

I ran an ad in *Philly Fit* magazine; a well-done, free publication. The magazine is distributed at health clubs, gyms, offices, businesses and spas. Advertising in this publication is an integral part of my External Marketing strategy.

I'd placed an ad that has a picture of me with the NBA Philadelphia Sixers Dancers, as I am the official cosmetic dentist of the dancers. I run the ad six to eight times a year. We always get people in from miles away, sometimes as far away as 30 miles.

Shortly after one of the Sixers Dancers ads ran, a young woman by the name of Jackie Restuccia made an appointment. The day before Jackie is scheduled I asked Theresa, my coordinator, "Where is this patient coming from and how old is she?" She said, "Hamilton, New Jersey. She's 20 years old." I'd never heard of Hamilton, New Jersey. Come to find out, it was almost two hours away. Most patients will only go a certain distance to see a dentist. Two hours is almost unheard of for a new patient.

I assumed because of Jackie's age and the fact we offer a discount of $250 with the ad, she was likely coming in for a whitening and not much else would need to be done.

The day of Jackie's appointment, I saw her and her mother walk into Theresa's room to fill out her medical history. Because I was in another room, I was not able to get a good look at either of them.

I overheard the conversation between my coordinator and Jackie and her mother. At one point Jackie said, "Oh, I forgot my coupon. Can I still get $250 off?" Finding myself prejudging the situation, I'm thinking, "Oh my gosh. *This* should be good."

A short while after Jackie was seated in my treatment room, I went in to meet and greet her. We as dentists have a habit that when we meet someone we look at teeth before we look at the person. If I meet someone new on the street, I can instantaneously tell you which tooth is crooked, which tooth has a filling, and which has a cap. We've been trained to look at teeth. It's second nature. We often do this before we look at a person's eyes.

Instinctively, I looked at Jackie's teeth. To say her teeth were not a pretty sight is an understatement. Nothing's in alignment, the front tooth is not the front tooth, there's a big tooth then small tooth, everything's crooked. I'm thinking, "Something major is wrong here."

Then I looked beyond her teeth, at her face. I saw her nose was not very straight and the point of her chin didn't line up with the midline of her face. Jackie is not a very big person; she almost looks miniaturized. My initial reaction was to assume she'd been in a car accident.

In that her mother appeared to be the one who was going to answer the initial questions, I asked Jackie's mother about her health. "Jackie was born with multiple birth issues. She has many midline defects. By that I mean the things that are in the middle of her body either didn't form or formed incompletely. One of the things that didn't form was her nose; she was born with no nose; she just had a hole.

"Her nose has been reconstructed over multiple surgeries. Although it's not perfectly straight, it's a nose. Jackie has had over 20 surgeries in her 20 years to correct some of her other issues," she said matter-of-factly. I sensed she had had this conversation with other professionals on many occasions.

I asked Jackie what she was thinking. She replied, "I've been to two dentists and an orthodontist and nobody can help me. They said that they can't do anything for me. They can't expand my pallet because I have no bone in the roof of my mouth."

Now that I knew this, I was curious how she ended up in my chair. "Well, what brought you here?" I inquired.

Without missing a beat she responded, "When I saw you were the Sixers Dancers' cosmetic dentists, I knew you could help me. If the Sixers Dancers let you fix their teeth, you could fix my teeth."

A bit taken aback by Jackie's reasoning, I was intrigued by the professional challenge and deeply touched by Jackie's dilemma.

Because of my training at the Las Vegas Institute of Advanced Dentistry and my own belief in my skill and expertise, I was confident I could help Jackie.

Looking gently into her eyes I said, "I think I can help you. I'll need to take some impressions of your mouth. We have to actually do this procedure on a model first in wax to see how much we can reposition your teeth and convert certain teeth to the right shape. Normally I don't do this step unless you're thinking about going ahead and a case like this is going to run about $15,000."

Jackie stared at her mother and her mother stared back at her. There was this gyration of an eye battle going on between the two of them. No one was saying anything.

In numerous sales courses I have taken over the years there is often a lesson taught about making the "pitch" and then keeping your mouth shut. For what seemed like well over a half-hour, I didn't talk and neither did they. Finally I said, "Well, look.

Let's just do this. Let's get the models and I'll give you an idea of what can be done. There will be no obligation on your part, but at least we can see what is possible." So I took the impressions and they left.

Something we do in my office is have team meetings on a daily basis. Occasionally we have a special meeting. Today called for just such a meeting. I shared with my team my experience with Jackie and her mom and asked them how they felt about the situation.

Here was a young woman who had been through more in her short 20 years than most people would go through in a lifetime and I just knew we had to do something. But I also knew I needed the full support and blessings from my team.

As fate would have it, my team and I had just returned from yet another training course at the Las Vegas Institute. During this particular visit to LVI we had made a commitment to donate a large-scale case each year. I felt Jackie definitely qualified as someone who would greatly benefit from us donating our services to her. As I began to share my thoughts with my team, several team members excitedly interrupted saying this was meant to be. As I was, they were convinced we had to do whatever we could to help Jackie.

This was to be our big contribution case for the year. With the kind of work Jackie needed it went beyond what we could do in the office. I also needed to enlist the help of a dental lab. I have worked with numerous labs over the years. One that stands head and shoulders above the rest is Becden Dental Lab located just outside of Salt Lake City, Utah. Becden was founded by Dennis and Becky Vasquez, two of the most giving and caring people I know.

I made a call to Becky. I asked if they were up for

contributing a significant case. Although they do a couple contribution cases a year, they had just done one. This was back in May and they weren't going to do another until September.

So rather than going into the details of Jackie's case, I emailed a picture of her to both Becky and Dennis. I also visualized them saying this was a case they wanted to contribute to. Upon seeing Jackie's picture, they immediately called to let me know they would do all the lab work at no charge.

Once again, I saw Charlie's teachings taking hold. Visualize what you want, believe it is possible, set the intention and take the action. Jackie's future was getting brighter by the moment.

Jackie and her mother returned a week later for her follow up consultation. I showed them the wax up and said, "This is what your teeth can look like."

With a slight gasp Jackie whispered, "Oh my God, that's beautiful." Her mother immediately said, "On the way down, I told Jackie we will find a way to afford this." She continued, "Unfortunately, a lot of the surgeries that Jackie has had are of a cosmetic nature and its all out-of-pocket money, but we will find a way to do this if you can help her."

Fighting to hold back my emotions, I looked first at Jackie, then at her mother and almost in a whisper said, "We've already discussed it. We've been very successful and we believe in giving back. We've decided to do this at no charge."

For a moment, I am sure you could have heard a pin drop. Then everyone began to cry. Jackie was crying and holding her mother. I'm crying holding the build up model. My assistants are crying, people on the other side of the office are crying, everybody's crying at this point. In that moment, I knew that I have been blessed beyond compare. To be able to be a part of a team that could make such an incredible difference in the life of someone like Jackie made me realize why achieving success and financial abundance has been a driving force for me. Ultimately, it is about contribution.

Jackie returned a week or two later for a four-hour visit to get her into temporaries. Because of the advances in cosmetic dentistry, in a matter of a few hours Jackie went from having crooked teeth to now having straight teeth.

For as long as I can remember, I have made it a practice to call a patient after a lengthy procedure. I like to know they are okay, check in with them and let them know I am there for them. That evening I called Jackie, but she didn't answer her phone. I called her back several times. When she finally answered, she sounded like she was crying. I asked if she was all right assuming she was in pain from all the work we had done.

Through the sobs she said, "I was crying."

Asking, "Well, why is that?"

She replied, "My grandmother said my nose doesn't look crooked anymore because my teeth are straight now. Dr. Capista, I love the way I look."

Little did Jackie know that when I hung up the phone tears filled my eyes. My wife came to me, hugged me and told me how proud she was of me. Feeling my emotions getting the better of me I told Anne, "We are so blessed to live the life we do." The blessings come from not only what I was able to do, but having people like my team, Becky and Dennis and all those who believe in contribution.

When Jackie came back and we put in her permanent teeth, it was a very happy day for our entire team. Not only were Jackie and her mother ecstatic with the results, our team was obviously touched and proud of the work we had done.

One of our team members said, "It makes me proud to work here." As connected as we already are, this event really brought us together even more as a team and as a family. All of us were lucky enough to share in an event that was life changing for one of our patients. Call it what you will, but I believe this whole experience was Divinely guided.

As I evaluate the experience, I can see the connection of everything. First, due to the way I market my practice, we had run a series of ads targeting cosmetic dentistry and mainly women. For whatever reason, whether it's an angel or just luck, Jackie saw the ad.

Because I work with the NBA Sixers Dancers, Jackie perceived me as an expert and someone that could help her. Because of this ad, we attracted a girl who drove almost two hours to our office with no understanding of our skill or expertise but with a goal in mind. She had a dream, a belief, and was willing to take the action. All she really wanted was simply to be able to smile.

There was no mistake in the fact that my team and I had recently decided to donate a large case. Knowing how life works, I knew the opportunity would present itself. That opportunity was Jackie. In my heart, I knew it from the moment I glanced at her crooked and missing teeth.

Believing in the power of asking and the goodness of others, when Becky and Dennis Vasquez were invited to participate in this experience, not only did they agree without any hesitation, so did their team. I found out later the technicians at Becden Lab actually took some of the work home and did it on their own time. This was a labor of love!

All the elements were falling into place for each of us to contribute in whatever way we could. No doubt all of us received much, much more by giving than Jackie received by getting a new smile. Beyond a shadow of a doubt, I know I did.

Although Jackie's case cost $15,000 of income, it was worth it. Money comes and goes. What was even more valuable than the money was the letter I received from Jackie's aunt. This letter has touched me to the core of who I am.

Dear Dr. Capista,

I am Jackie Restuccia's aunt and also her godmother. As you found out for yourself, she is one special young lady. I felt I needed to reach out to you to express how wonderful your pure act of goodness and kindness impacted my niece, my sister and our entire family.

I don't need to get into details, because you already know what Jackie and my sister have been through, but I'm sure you realize how your gesture of compassion has made them both feel. I know that on a personal level you have restored, or should I say, reconfirmed my belief and faith in humanity.

I wanted to personally thank you for helping my niece achieve a beautiful smile that reflects the beautiful and lovely young lady she is inside. And for giving back to my sister in this special way because she has a huge heart and is always doing things for others. She is truly deserving of your kindness.

Please know that I will think of you often. When I hear of other acts of kindness I will think of you. And when I hear of acts of inhumanity, I will think of you and remember there is good in this world. That we all need each other and that one life can touch so many others without even know they have done so. I have shared this story with many of my friends and you have touched each one of their lives in a very special way.

With all my heart I thank you for this wonderful gift you have given my niece and I will keep you in my thoughts and prayers always.

Janice A. Eckstein

I believe we are all meant to do wonderful things in life. Often what we are called to do is something small, other times not. The fact is, it can be something as simple as sharing time with another, or helping a friend in need, or in my case, making one woman's life better with a beautiful smile.

Unfortunately, we may lose sight of our purpose because we may not realize how much of what we do can forever change the path of another. Or we get caught up in trying to analyze what our purpose is. The fact is, our purpose is to be of service.

If ever I wonder if I am doing what I was meant to do, all I have to do is read the letter. I keep that letter on my desk and I will read it today, tomorrow, next week, next month, next year, ten years from now and get a feeling that I couldn't buy. I call this letter my *Million-Dollar Letter* because that's what it is worth to me.

So if you look at it, this letter cost me $15,000. The cost is insignificant compared to the feeling I get every time I read it; it's priceless. Not a day goes by that I don't read the letter and immediately get a shift in my feelings, perception and level of gratitude.

What would you pay to have something you could keep nearby that can immediately transform you from being in a bad mood to feeling good again? From feeling so-so to an incredible level of gratitude? From wondering if what you do is making a difference to *knowing* you are making a difference?

What has really hit home for me with this experience is that I couldn't do this kind of giving if I wasn't profitable and successful. Simple as that. No beating around the bush on this one. In order to give at a high level, you absolutely must be successful and profitable. Again, *you cannot give what you do not have*. If you cannot meet payroll and have a certain level of profitability, you cannot give back.

This is what drives me to teach people about success and building their own business. The more we have the more we can give to others.

When people hold beliefs about money and success that prevent them from being in a position to contribute, I have to wonder why. If, through my presentations, my daily interactions, my mentoring, this book or any number of ways I can impact the way a person views success, then I have done my job.

One of the greatest things you can do is to make contributing a part of your business practice. You have an obligation to be profitable in your business if you want to do something like this. That obligation is to you, your family, your team, your community, your church, and the organizations you believe in. If you contribute some of your income, you're the one that receives the most, but you can't do it if you're not profitable.

When working with Jackie, I also felt the satisfaction of actually working with her, giving my time and sweat, and creating something lasting for her. Giving money is satisfying; working with someone creates a deeper satisfaction. Jackie, her mom, my team and I spent many hours together co-creating for a better life.

People who have a lot of money tend to give money as their form of contribution. Although giving money is great, it is when you have to actually sit down and perform a service that you feel a different energy involved.

Whatever you decide to do, do it from the heart. It always, always comes back to you tenfold. That is one of the oldest principles of abundance and success you will find.

I know I make more money by giving than if I didn't give. Yet, I don't give for the purpose of how much I get in return. I do it because it is the right thing to do.

I know people find us because of what we do and who we are. The number of people affected by Jackie's story is something we will never know for sure. All of Jackie's co-workers were overwhelmed by the experience as well as Jackie's family, friends and distant relatives being affected in a very positive way. Although I do not use Jackie's story as a marketing tool to get new patients, I do know the Universe seems to reward unconditional service.

Becden Lab received letters of thanks and photographs of Jackie. As I said, some of their employees took their work home so they could contribute on their own time. I think there was a lot of divine guidance concerning Jackie's case.

Sometimes I wonder why someone would drive two hours to a dental office based on a Sixers Dancers ad. I think things happen for a reason. Jackie was guided to our office; we were guided to help her. I believe we are guided and presented with opportunities all the time. Whether it's an energy or a force of God is a mystery. What we do with these opportunities is up to us. One thing I know for sure is that by being a blessing to others we open ourselves up to being blessed.

A huge lesson here is to trust that guiding force. When you are moved to take a step in a certain direction, take the step. Then the next. And the next. And still the next.

You won't know until you start doing these things what synergy helping others creates. In most cases, teeth are not a life and death issue, but they can make or break a personality or affect someone's life in other ways. Sometimes death can be a simple thing compared to living your life in misery. I think Jackie was not a happy person with the way she looked because of her physical challenges.

Now that she has a beautiful smile, she finally has something attractive people can focus on. I think this has had a big influence on her. Everyone involved was rewarded. I feel like I received the greatest reward because I was the service provider, yet the others involved in the experience likely feel their own rewards. And I know I could have not done this alone. It took everyone to create the miracle.

I think Jackie and her family who lived the *Before* and rejoice in the *After* will be forever grateful. That is more than enough for me.

I know people who have and give lots of money away. In many ways, this is much easier than going out and spending the whole weekend in a soup kitchen or doing something that requires time. Volunteering at a soup kitchen could be a different way of giving and generally a much harder thing to do. I liken it to Jackie's case, providing hours of dental care for Jackie was much more challenging than just making a financial contribution. And like I said, much, much more rewarding.

If I were 30 years old, I probably would not have done this. Actually, at 30 I was not as skilled as I am today, nor would I have felt the same depth of meaning and satisfaction. Something like this, an act of charity, contributes to self-love, which gives you the ability to love other people in a greater way.

The Million-Dollar Letter helps me feel better about myself. That's why I said I really believe I received much more by giving than even Jackie did by getting a few thousand dollars worth of teeth.

No matter how successful we become, there are days you can feel beat up and there are days you feel things aren't going the way you want them to, or you don't feel good about yourself. Then you read something like the *Million Dollar Letter* and it changes everything. If you're not feeling good on the inside, it's pretty hard to perform on the outside. This letter gets inside you and makes you feel better.

If you choose success for success' sake, it will always be fleeting. If you choose success to contribute and impact the lives of others with great scale, you will leave a legacy of love for many years to come.

If you want to experience success on the deepest level, find ways to contribute. Do so with no intention of getting anything in return. It is when you contribute with no strings attached you receive blessings beyond your wildest imagination.

MILLION-DOLLAR LETTER
SUCCESS SUMMARY

1. Acts of kindness impact many people, not just the one giving or receiving.
2. Give of your services not just your money.
3. The more success you experience the more you can give.
4. You need to be profitable in order to give back.
5. When you willingly give and give freely to the places you are called to give to, the more you receive; not just tenfold, but twenty, thirty, even a hundred fold.
6. Giving allows you to realign your purpose of sharing your abundance.
7. You often receive more by giving than the person you give to.
8. To experience success on the deepest level, find ways to contribute.

9. When you are moved to take a step in a certain direction, take the step. Then the next. And the next. And still the next.

CHAPTER 13

My Vision for the Future

When I think about what the potential for the future is, I get very excited and often become very emotional. I think back to what it was like to be that ten-year-old kid who knew what he wanted; a kid who was told to change his goal. A kid who just knew that wasn't the way it was supposed to be.

Because I stayed true to my vision, had the good fortune of meeting Charlie, was open to other mentors, teachings and spiritual practices, today I have no doubt whatsoever that I am living the life I was intended to live.

The more I learn the truth, the more I have the urge and desire to try to tell other people what I've been told. The truth is, you can have, be and do whatever you want, if you want it bad enough.

I still love being a dentist and I still want to be a dentist, but after over 30 years of owning my own business, drilling on teeth and enjoying the success I now enjoy, I realize it is time for me to share my knowledge with as many people as I can.

As I talk to people who don't know many of the tools and techniques that I've been privy to and have had the great fortune to learn, I am compelled to pass this on and teach other people. I get a big kick out of seeing people who know nothing, or very little about this way of living, start to use the program and watch it help their life.

One of the most profound examples of someone who lived their dream by believing in themselves is the story about Jason McElwain, an autistic teen. Jason has been involved with his high school basketball team for years and was an acting manager. Without fail, he showed up to every game and did what he could to support the team. Having never played a game, he was asked to suit up for the season's last game. With only minutes remaining in the game, the coach put him in just so he could have the experience.

For Jason, this was not about an experience, but a dream come true. With the love and support of his team members, he attempted a basket, only to watch the ball bounce off the rim. A few seconds later he got the ball again, made another attempt and missed.

Then something magical happened. In a matter of minutes Jason scored 20 points. Never in the history of the team had any player, even the star player, done this. With his classmates and teammates cheering wildly, Jason fulfilled his lifelong dream in front of hundreds of people. Since that time, the video of his miraculous experience has been viewed by millions.

Some might call Jason lucky. The way Jason explains it

confirms how powerful beliefs, thoughts and actions are.

"After I made the first basket, the basket became as big as a big 'ole bucket. I felt like I was shooting free throws."

I can equate that to business. I may have taken many shots and missed a bunch of them, but as more shots went in, the basket got bigger and my successes got easier.

Something else important about Jason's story is that Jason would practice for hours on end by himself, shooting basket after basket after basket. It wasn't luck that allowed him to fulfill his dream, and it won't be luck in your business that creates your success. Sure, maybe there is an element of luck in everything, but I believe luck is more about being willing to do what has to be done and preparing for opportunity to arrive.

As I told my good friend and accountant, David Haines, more than once, my goal is not necessarily to be the richest dentist in the world, but I want to be the happiest dentist *and* person in the world. I think by doing these things, it makes me happier to help other people in that respect.

At first, I was not sure David understood what I meant. Being a person whose job it is to help his clients achieve financial goals and David being very much an analytic type, there were times I know David thought I might be getting sidetracked by my speaking and non-dental adventures. Yet there have been many occasions in recent years when David has told me how much what I have shared with him has enhanced his life. I have learned from him and he from me. Over the last eight years, we have talked at least once a week, sometimes about business, sometimes about life, just as Charlie and I did, and over that time, we have mentored each other.

Although I get paid to teach professionals this information, there are times I choose not to get paid. I so love what I do that I fully understand what it means when people say, "If you would do what you get paid to do for free, you know you are on your path."

When I am invited to speak to a group of college kids about their life and about business, I get a huge kick out of that. It may sound cliché, but if I can touch one person, I have succeeded.

When I have the opportunity to mentor highly successful executives, who are intelligent, smart people, and I watch their eyes light up the way mine have for years with Charlie, I have succeeded.

For example, one person I mentor, who is the vice president of a very powerful organization, looks at me and gets very excited when he says, "Wow, this is great stuff. I have to do this, I have to do this!" He does it and that puts a smile on my face.

Although today most of this information is very obvious to me, it's not so obvious to a lot of other people. Like me over 30 years ago, many people "just didn't know what they didn't know."

I see living my life and teaching others like Charlie has done for years until I can't walk. You know, he's almost 90 years old and he's still pushing me and encouraging me to expand myself.

To this day he inspires me as much as the first time I heard him share his wisdom. My ultimate goal is to be a resource to other people just like Charlie has been.

Thanks, Charlie.

MY VISION FOR THE FUTURE
SUCCESS SUMMARY

1. You have to take shots to make baskets and they do not all go in.
2. As you make the baskets and have successes, the future successes happen easier.
3. Luck doesn't get you success. It comes from hard work and practice.
4. Pass on to others what you know and what has made you successful.
5. There is always more to learn and pass on to others.

Conclusion

Simple is not Always Easy

Most of what you need for success is simple, but not necessarily easy. As I previously mentioned, successful people are willing to do what unsuccessful people will not. Successful people are willing to invest the time, effort and money to create the life they want.

I equate it to riding a bike. Riding a bike is simple, but it's not easy when you first start out. Sure, it's easy if you've been doing it for a while. Once you learn how to ride, even when you take a break from riding your body retains the memory — hence the term, "It's like riding a bike; you never forget."

If you've never ridden a bike before, it isn't that easy the first time — it is very difficult. Likewise, the things I have asked you to do to achieve *TOTAL SUCCESS* are simple, but not always easy. They can, however, give you an *incredible* life. That is why I wrote this book. To help anyone who wants it bad enough to achieve *TOTAL SUCCESS*.

What has been discussed throughout this book is the importance of having systems to obtain predictable and consistent results in business and personal life. We also talked about the need to focus on the big picture of the relationship of your Product or Service to Internal Marketing and External Marketing and the relationship of these to your Sales Call and your Sales Presentation.

Additionally, we talked about the importance of having and using mentors, controlling your thoughts and balance in life. You learned how balance in your personal life can affect success in your business as well as about the relationship of having balance in your life in order to achieve *TOTAL SUCCESS*.

As I stated, I had certain objectives for you with this book. They are to have:

- Easy to understand and apply principles to grow your business.
- Principles based on systems to have success in your business.
- Principles based on systems to improve your personal life.
- The skills and resources to achieve *TOTAL SUCCESS* and have a happy life.
- The willingness to "get it" and "do it."

Because you have stuck around to this point it means you really do want success. Now it's up to you. If you only read the book and don't apply at least some of it, this just means you would rather talk about success than have it. Sadly, that is what the majority of people will do their entire lives. They settle for mediocrity.

To avoid this go back and try these things. Maybe not everything is going to work the first time. Maybe it won't work the second time, but you have to keep trying. There is no excuse for not achieving success. Look at Jason McElwain. Even though he had the deck stacked against him, he didn't use that as an excuse not to fulfill his dream.

And even though Jason missed his first few shots, he kept taking the shots. He kept at it until he achieved success.

The people who are going to enjoy a life of *TOTAL SUCCESS* are those who are tired of the BS and are willing to do what it takes. They are willing to take shot after shot. Just as Jason missed a few shots, I want you to go back to your business and your life and take some shots. Even if you miss, you have to keep going. As Charlie says, "You can have anything in life if you want it badly enough and are willing to pay the price."

So by now I hope you "get it" and go DO IT! I'm not kidding, you have to *do it*. And to do it you have to *get it*.

If you want *TOTAL SUCCESS* take the shot!

RECOMMENDED RESOURCES

BOOKS

- ✓ *Lead the Field* and *The Strangest Secret* — Earl Nightingale
- ✓ *How to Stay Motivated* and *See You at the Top* — Zig Ziglar
- ✓ *The Psychology of a Winner* — Denis Waitley
- ✓ *Think and Grow Rich* — Napolian Hill
- ✓ *The Greatest Salesman in the World* — Og Mandino
- ✓ *The Psychology of Achievement* — Brian Tracy
- ✓ *As a Man Thinketh* — James Allen
- ✓ *How to Win Friends and Influence People* — Dale Carnegie
- ✓ *The Richest Man in Babylon* — George S. Clason

CDs

- ✓ *Lead the Field* and *The Strangest Secret* — Earl Nightingale

TRAINING MATERIAL

- ✓ DiSC® Classic by Inscape Publishing
- ✓ Adventures in Attitudes® by Inscape Publishing
- ✓ Sales and Marketing Training — Dr. Joe Capista

Visit www.joecapista.com or
www.thesuccesstriangle.com
to access all DISC® Classic and
other recommended resources.

About the Author

Dr. Joe Capista

 Dr. Joe Capista is recognized for his unique approach to business, life and success. As the owner of one of the most successful dental practices in the United States, Dr. Joe Capista has an exceptional understanding of what it takes to create a successful business and a successful life while maintaining balance both personally and professionally to create *TOTAL SUCCESS*.

Dr. Capista oversees operations for Williamsburg Dental, a multi-million dollar practice with two locations in the Delaware County, Pennsylvania metropolitan area.

Williamsburg Dental has been serving clients for over 25

years and has an outstanding reputation for quality patient care. Dr. Capista and his entire team deliver the most advanced, proven dental treatments to their patients. Dr. Capista is The Cosmetic Dentist for the NBA Philadelphia Sixers Dance Team.

For over two decades, Dr. Capista has been on the leading edge of business trends including understanding what drives your team to perform at top level, what motivates a client and customer to do business with you and how to create a life most only dream of.

His unique approach to marketing a business is fast becoming a highly sought out strategy by numerous types and sizes of businesses. Joe combines a unique understanding of the workplace, personal development, implementation of effective systems, overall balance and possibility into all he does.

He is highly recognized for his ability to teach clients how to maximize dollars for both Internal and External Marketing in order that they gain optimum results.

Dr. Capista has successfully incorporated overseeing operations for his business into being a highly requested speaker and trainer. A content driven, inspirational speaker, Joe makes audiences think and leaves them wanting more. His message is simple: be committed, do what you love, love what you do, live with passion, give back to your community, and create balance in all areas of your life to enjoy a life beyond your wildest dreams.

Dr. Capista presents to groups ranging from small business owners to CEOs of Fortune 100 corporations. His easygoing presentation style makes him an audience favorite.

Dr. Capista received his Bachelor of Science degree in Biology from LaSalle University and went on to earn his Doctor of Dental Surgery (DDS) from Temple University School of Dentistry in 1976. He completed a general practice residency at

Philadelphia General Hospital.

Dr. Capista is a respected authority on aesthetic dentistry and conducts seminars throughout the region on the latest cosmetic and restorative techniques. Dr. Capista has completed training at the renowned Las Vegas Institute of Advanced Dental Studies.

He is a member of the American Dental Association; the Pennsylvania Dental Association, the American Academy of Cosmetic Dentistry and the Chester/Delaware County Dental Association.

Dr. Joe Capista, the author of
***What Can a Dentist Teach You
about Business, Life and Success?***
is available for keynote speaking
engagements and training.

To learn more about all of Dr. Capista's services visit:
www.joecapista.com

To order this book in quantity call our
Sales Department at:
541.654.0426

Or mail:
Dr. Joe Capista
The Success Triangle™
P.O. Box 2007
Media, PA 19063